INSPIRED (

RICHARD BAXTER TOWNSHEND
('RBT' of the *Enigma* Variations)

TRANSCRIBED AND EDITED,
WITH SOME ELGARIAN INTERLUDES,
BY
KEVIN ALLEN

For Pete, Elgarian and Golfer.

'Right through the ages the mightiest brains have occupied
themselves with this noble sport.'
-P. G. Wodehouse

© Kevin Allen, 2004
First published in this edition 2004.
Inspired Golf, by R. B. Townshend, Transcribed and Edited with some
Elgarian Interludes

ISBN: 0-9531227-3-5

Further copies are available from the author at
2, Milford Court,
Gale Moor Avenue,
Alverstoke,
GOSPORT,
Hampshire,
PO12 2TN,
at £7.50 per copy plus £1.00 p&p UK and Europe,
£2.00 Rest of World.

Printed in Great Britain by
Aspect Design and Print
89, Newtown Road
Malvern,
Worcs.
WR14 1PD

CONTENTS

ILLUSTRATIONS

Front cover:
'For those in peril on the tee' – Elgar driving at Stoke Prior, c. 1895

Frontispiece:
RBT demonstrating the lasso in his Oxford garden

Photographs between pages 34 and 53 :-
1. 'Eye on the ball' – Elgar inspires at Hasfield Court
2. Bernard Keeling, RBT's great-nephew, astride his wooden horse
3. Elgar's golfing friends – F. A. Horn, Chairman of the Green Committee, with the Club's professional, G. H. Cawsey, apparently summoned from behind the bar...
4. ...G. D. Carr, Secretary for many years
5. ...and W. Paterson, Secretary 1900
6. 'Made probably on the golf links' – music for *The Dream of Gerontius*
7. A plan of the Worcestershire Club Course as it was during Elgar's membership
8. Off to the Links - Elgar and plus-fours at 'Craeg Lea,' 1903
9. The composer putting, with Carice poised to replace the flag
10. The route to the Links ? – a street map of Malvern, c.1902
11. The Club House, with caddies in attendance
12. A drive at the ninth
13. A three-ball match at the tenth
14. The thirteenth tee – and railway lines
15. Paterson at the fourteenth, with Malvern College in the background
16. A drive at the fifteenth
17. Amaryllis in the Garden? A sketch from the Norbury papers
18. The Ladies' Club House
    ENDPIECE: The Malvern Hills from the Old Golf Course

Back cover:
Elgar at Stoke, about to 'smite the knave'

By the same author:

Elgar the Cyclist: A Creative Odyssey

Elgar in Love: Vera Hockman and the Third Symphony

August Jaeger, Portrait of Nimrod: A Life in Letters and Other Writings (Ashgate Press)

(Available from the Elgar Birthplace Museum, www.elgarmuseum.org • Tel: 01905 333224)

In preparation:

Gracious Ladies: The Norbury Family and Edward Elgar

Other books by Richard Baxter Townshend:

Col. Richard Townesend of Casteltown: An Officer of the Long Parliament and His Descendants. Frowde, 1892 (with Dorothea Townshend)

Tacitus: The Agricola and Germania. (Translated) Methuen, 1894

Lone Pine, a novel. Methuen, 1899 reprinted 1913

The Bride of a Day, a novel. George Allen, 1905. (With Dorothea Townshend)

The Complete Air-Gunner. Upcott Gill, 1907 (Reprinted by Hiller Publications, 1984)

Gunpowder, Treason and Plot, and Other Stories, with H. Avery & F. Whishaw, Nelson 1911

A Girl from Mexico, a novel. Methuen, 1914

A Tenderfoot in Colorado. John Lane 1923

The Tenderfoot in New Mexico. John Lane 1923

Bullwhack Joe, the Yarns of a Tenderfoot. John Lane 1925

Last Memories of a Tenderfoot. John Lane 1926

A MILLION TO ONE

Hurrah for the tee's flat stand,
Your ball on its pinch of sand,
The slow back swing,
The loose wrist fling,
And the drive which is simply grand!

Hurrah for that second clean
From a lie just fit for a queen
With the best club you've got,
When a lightning shot
Lays the ball right there on the green!

Hurrah for the long putt free,
The putt that's meant to be
Down all the way,
Let come what may;
And that four hole done in three!

Ah would it were ever thus,
When you never need make a fuss
Bunkered heavy in sand,
Other bunkers at hand,
And nothing to do but cuss.

You count up your hopeless score:
Already you've played two more:
Your opponent grins
While you think of your sins,
But remember you've been there before!

And miracles happen in golf
Sometimes even when you are off;
It's a million to one,
Yet the thing has been done,
Holing out with a niblick loft.

Then here's to the glorious game
That never twice is the same;
May we all of us play
Till our final day
And then not fail of our aim.

Richard Baxter Townshend

Frontispiece: RBT demonstrating the lasso in his Oxford garden
(From *A Tenderfoot in Colorado*)

A Note on the Author

A real Victorian man of many, not to say contrasting, parts, Richard Baxter Townshend (1846 – 1923) came from an old Irish family with an estate in County Cork. He was educated at Repton School and Trinity College, Cambridge, where he read Classics, rowed for the First Boat Club and became a member of 'Magpie & Stump,' the Debating Society. Mindful perhaps of his lack of an inheritance as a younger son, he went out to the United States at the age of twenty-three, 'roughing it' as a cattle-rancher, gold-prospector and trader in horses and mules. In all he spent ten years in the West, experiencing many hardships and adventures including a meeting with Billy the Kid. Despite his success in a man's world, Townshend was remarkable for his somewhat feminine appearance. He had rosy cheeks and blue eyes, a high-pitched voice and a love of unusual clothes; his college nickname had been 'cherub.'

Having made his pile in America, he returned to England and took a teaching post at Bath College. His connection with the Elgar circle began with his marriage to Dorothea Baker, a sister of his University friend William Meath Baker, of Hasfield Court, Gloucestershire. Dorothea's elder sister, Mary Frances, or Minnie, was a close friend of Alice Roberts, who would marry the composer in 1889. Townshend quitted his teaching at Bath after five years and in 1891 moved to Oxford where he spent the rest of his life. Here he returned to scholarship and published translations of the Classics, many vivid articles describing his 'Wild West' days, (later published in book form), adventure stories and sporting books. In a city famed for eccentrics, he became a noted one, writing at his study desk sitting in a specially constructed saddle and riding around Oxford on a tricycle fitted with a continuously ringing bell. Somewhat deaf, he felt the bell helped other people to hear him coming, as he couldn't hear them. Those of us who have narrowly escaped onslaught by bicycle in Oxford can only suggest that the idea is long overdue for renewal.

Townshend described his American days with a scholar's commitment and he remains not without importance as a historian of the West. Many of his photographs of various Indian tribes and their ceremonies have been preserved at the Pitt Rivers Museum in Oxford and the Royal Anthropological Institute in London. Dorothea also turned to authorship, producing historical works and stories for girls, and occasionally collaborating with her husband on larger joint projects.

After his marriage Elgar met the cowboy-scholar frequently at Hasfield Court and the two unconventional men struck up a rapport. Townshend's unusual background would have been of much interest to the composer and it is easy to imagine him preferring the older man's many racy yarns of American adventure to the polite tea-time conversations of the Baker ladies. But it did not stop there. As the man who, as their friendship developed, taught Elgar to play golf, Townshend did more for English music than he knew; he was rewarded by inclusion in the musical portrait-gallery which was the composer's first great work, the 'Enigma' Variations. His music, the third variation of the set, is titled simply 'R.B.T.' In its affectionate caricature of his various mannerisms, the movement pays tribute to a loyal supporter and adds further lustre to the name of a remarkable man.

Townshend first began to teach Elgar golf on 23rd December, 1892, during a Christmas house-party at Hasfield Court; the magnificent house had extensive grounds where the *game could easily be played. No doubt the beginner was shown how to take a swing at a daisy, and told of the 'eye on the ball' and 'head as still as possible' maxims, among the many others that Townshend includes in the first chapter of his book. But perhaps it was his main theory of breathing synchronised with the swing – 'inspired golf' – that formed the basis of that first lesson. If so, it would have been most appropriate. We talk about composers having an 'inspiration,' a sudden, brilliant idea. But it cannot be mere coincidence that the word also refers to the drawing-in of a breath, with accompanying positive feelings of well-being and pleasurable anticipation. Those golf lessons at Hasfield went so well that they continued on Christmas Eve and Boxing Day; Christmas Day had other distractions of course but even so Elgar and Townshsend managed to get out for a walk, during which, as Alice Elgar's diary tells us, they 'found golf balls,' evidence perhaps of Elgar's necessarily inexpert activities with the club of the preceding days.*

*

So let us proceed to Townshend's opening chapter with its introduction of the idea of 'inspiration' alongside reminders of all the standard procedures. After a page or two it is not difficult to imagine that we are listening to the voice of the man himself, for he addresses the reader directly and informally. We feel that we are listening to an accomplished teacher, full of no-nonsense practical advice, who knows the importance of taking one step at a time and of being aware of the feelings of the golfing devotee anxious to improve his game. His instructions throughout are full of humour, analogy and example drawn from his own varied experiences. There cannot be many golfing manuals which draw on classical French and Latin literature on the one hand, and penitential self-flagellation on the other, and manage to be so effective a vehicle of instruction.

CHAPTER 1: THE SIN OF ACEDIA

This little work is a humble attempt to come to the rescue of the golfing backslider. The backslider may be taken to be a player who, after having been for some time familiar with the game of golf, finds himself (or herself) slipping steadily back instead of forwards, which for a keen hand is a truly miserable state to fall into. The victim of the lapse is quite aware that something or other has gone radically wrong with his golf, and yet he is quite unable to discover what is the matter. He tries desperately hard to cure himself, only to find that he grows more and more uncertain of his stroke; and in this unhappy condition he is apt to fall into the sin of acedia. Acedia is an old monkish term for a spiritual numbness, a sort of dull acceptance of the fatal feeling that nothing is or can be of any use. When this state of acedia proves to be chronic, as too often happens, the victim sees an awful future before him; he sees himself as a weak and erring brother, knowing that such he must ever be, and, worst of all, not caring.

Take heart, poor victim! Others before you have suffered, and some at least have found out what to them has opened a way of escape. Try, at any rate, the simple remedy I offer. You can fall no lower than you are; you may take a turn for the better. And with my very best wishes for your salvation I plunge in medias res.

I take for granted that (like myself) you are either a regular double-figure handicap man or else your backsliding has brought you so low that your allowance ought to be reckoned in double figures, and that, in short, your present plight is such as to leave you not the shadow of a chance against a scratch player unless he concedes you a dozen strokes or more. Take yourself as such then; and now you need not be too proud to condescend to the comforting assistance of a liberal tee. A tee only a single millimetre in height may suit the ideal of the plus handicap man, the great artist in golf; and if it pleases you to imitate him do so; but remember that for you his ideal method may prove only a hindrance, just as of old the armour of Saul was to David. You know yourself for a weak brother; very well, then, accept the fact, and do not be afraid to accept anything that helps your weakness. The plus man, as I said, may tee up his ball only one millimetre or the twenty-fifth part of an inch. Do you tee up yours a quarter of an inch, a half inch, a whole inch, nay two inches even, if by any means you can but give yourself the confidence that you are not going either to top it or to schlaff. Take a club, take any club you like, driver, brassy, cleek, iron, stand six feet back from the ball, and try a preliminary swing at a daisy: if there are no daisies a scrap of paper or a gun-wad will do as well. Address your daisy, and waggle as much as you like. Even a weak brother (or sister) has the right to waggle every bit as well and every bit as much as the plus player. While you waggle watch your breathing, watch just how you draw the air into your lungs and exhale it again. Now inhale deeply, then exhale, waggling all the time, and as you finish exhaling sole your club behind the daisy. Keep the club soled a moment while you draw in a full inspiration, shut your lips tight, and hold your breath. Now, now – instantly but slowly – take the club up – still holding the breath – up to the top of the swing, pause there for the barest fraction of a second, and then swiftly deliver the blow. Not till the club comes away after passing the daisy are you to let your breath go out fully and freely. This is the inspiration I speak of, this delivery of the blow when the lungs are filled with air and the breath is held. Here is the secret out at last. Practise it, yes, practise it assiduously, with faith and hope, and what before seemed impossible will come easy to you. You will cease to slide backwards; you will be another golfer, a new man.

There is no mystery about the thing, no faking, no doping, no magic. It is no mechanical trick of a fancy club fitted with a concealed spring, or of a new ball filled with something more elastic than rubber. The secret is in you, in yourself. Here, inside your chest, you have lungs; fill them, and strike with them filled. There you have it! You cannot believe in so simple a remedy? Try it.

Of course, inspiration does not supersede all the knowledge, the painfully hard-won knowledge, of golf which you already possess. For the most part the old maxims that you have so often repeated to yourself were true before, and they remain as true as ever still. Take only a few of them:

1. Eye on the ball.
2. Slow back.
3. Start the club up with the wrists.
4. Left wrist hollow not arched.
5. Grip with the fingers.
6. Grip tight with the left.
7. Grip tighter in the down swing.
8. Upper arms near the body.
9. Left hip well round towards the ball.
10. Left shoulder well down to the ball.
11. Backbone the axis of swing.
12. Head as still as possible.
13. Follow through with the arms.
14. Hands away.
15. Left foot at finish firm on the ground.

Well, there are fifteen of them, anyway, to be thought of at once and consecutively; they might easily be multiplied to a full hundred, a figure enough to make the golfer recall the predicament of the unfortunate insect with her hundred legs:

The centipede was happy quite
Until the toad in fun
Said, 'Pray which leg goes after which?'
And worked her mind to such a pitch
She lay distracted in the ditch
Considering how to run.

The golfer's grip of the stance with his feet has been described as almost quadrumanous, but his brain has to work more like clockwork even than a centipede's. Moreover the fifteen maxims above cited are all positive commandments, all 'thou-shalts'; of 'thou-shalt-nots' the list is just as long: don't press . . . don't sway . . . and so forth.

But there, never mind the number, and don't let them worry you; have faith in inspiration, and go on swinging cheerfully at the modest daisies on your lawn. I say on your lawn, for that is the sort of quiet place where you should first practise inspiration, if the idea, as I assume, be new to your mind. For Heaven's sake do give the new idea a fair chance and don't let it run away with you; don't go off at once to make a match with a friend and proceed to play round with the notion that this novelty of inspiration is going to do you a lot of good. The novelty will infallibly thrust all the older ideas into the background, and though you may have been badly off your game before you may find there are lower depths still to which you can fall, which is very far from the result I am aiming at.

No, the new idea must be introduced discreetly and without disturbance to the great company of ideas already huddling together in the dimly lit chambers of your inner self. I sincerely hope that inspiration will prove a godsend to you, but the pressing need is to prevent it from becoming a curse and upsetting your poor bewildered brain worse than the centipede's. How to solve this problem will be the next point that we have to consider.

O Hearken Thou

Interlude: 'You have this day been elected a member . . .'

Those first lessons with RBT drew an immediate response from Elgar, and over the next eleven years, until he left Malvern in 1904, the composer would play the game with something amounting to fanaticism, although he never became a great golfer. His view was that 'if not of the first force, he was certainly animated by the best of intentions.' His real talents were of course elsewhere, and these were exactly the years that saw Elgar rise from the life of a provincial music teacher who composed in his spare time, to a position of great musical distinction, a knighthood, and world fame.

Early in the new year of 1893, Elgar bought some clubs and some new clothes, presumably for outdoor wear, including gaiters to protect his trousers. Next on the agenda was the problem of finding somewhere to play, a matter which in the event was arranged with gratifying, and perhaps surprising, speed. The solution lay very much to hand, for Malvern was the home of the Worcestershire Golf Club. But would such a stronghold of the local establishment happily admit such a socially inferior person as a music-teacher? Exactly what was said during the Membership Committee's deliberations we shall never know, but it seems that they would, for on 22nd March George Jones, Club Secretary, wrote to Elgar that he had 'the pleasure of informing you that you have this day been elected a Member . . . and I enclose herewith a Book of Rules and a List of Members.'

There was also the matter of the entrance fee and subscription, four guineas altogether, no small amount for Elgar in those days, when his fee for a whole term's violin lessons might be three guineas. The money was payable to the Club's Treasurer, a certain Henry Dyke Acland, who has not yet perhaps received the recognition he deserves for the significant role he played in the frequently difficult days of the composer's early career. As an amateur cellist Acland, somebody who moved in local musical circles, was no doubt already a friend of Elgar, who by that time was very well-known in the area not only as a teacher but as a performer, conductor, arranger and general odd-job man of music, with, bye-the-bye, a few rather good compositions to his credit. For one thing, Acland must surely have known of the splendid concert-overture 'Froissart' which had been performed at the Worcester Three Choirs Festival some three years before, nearly fifteen minutes of stirring, surging orchestral music the like of which no other local composer could have produced. It must have been obvious that here was a man who could go places, given the chance, and it may well have been Acland's influence which helped to secure the composer's election to the Club. The Manager of Malvern's Old Bank, Acland was a person worth knowing, and he seems to have been a man of genuine culture from a distinguished background. A solid Churchman and Chairman of the Malvern Ratepayers Association, Acland was a son of Sir Henry Wentworth Dyke Acland, an Oxford Professor of Anatomy and former Physician to the Queen; he was a godson of John Ruskin and became a Fellow of the Geographical Society. As the son of a Worcester tradesman, Elgar must have been grateful for the opportunities the Club gave him to meet and mix with the movers and shakers of local society. Malvern's social snobbery could be nothing short of cruel at times and Elgar, whose father kept a shop and tuned pianos, well knew what it was to be 'cut' on account of his profession no less than his class; perhaps indeed they were almost one and the same thing.

Founded in 1879, the Worcestershire Golf Club exuded the influence of the aristocracy and gentry. Its first Presidents were Earl Beauchamp, the Earl of Coventry and Lord Lyttleton, and its Committee and membership were thick with Honourables, Majors, Colonels and Reverends. It was sited on a stretch of land at Malvern Wells, usually known now as Peachfield Common, but named Malvern Common on the Ordnance Survey Map, affording splendid, dramatic views along almost the whole range of the celebrated Malvern Hills. A railway station was conveniently close, and such was the influence of the golfing classes of those days that special fares and timetable alterations were negotiable on behalf of the Worcester members. As it grew the Club was able to engage a professional and build a caddies' shed and a rather grand Club House, gradually enlarged to include servants' quarters, a committee room, a dining room, a drying room, lockers and the usual conveniences. Cigars and cigarettes were on sale. The only problem seemed to be the well, which is still present inside the building today. The water became smelly and was found to contain 'worms and polywogs,' before being put right.

Originally just a 12-hole affair, the course was later extended to two nines, divided between railway lines, as there were in fact two stations at the Wells, operated by two different companies. Despite its magnificent location, the course, being on common land, suffered from poor drainage and any number of awkward lies due to wheel and hoof tracks and animal droppings. It was a hard school in which to develop one's game. Although there were no bunkers there were any number of natural hazards such as roads, ditches and gorse bushes as well of course as the railway lines. The 'Illustrated Sporting and Dramatic News' for October 1900 wrote 'The turf is of that springy nature to be found only on old common land; and given a fair amount of luck, a driver can nearly always be used in place of a brassy for the second shot to the long holes. One feature of the links, due to the clay soil, is the deadness of the greens in wet weather and their fieriness in summer.' In fact the Club was forced to promulgate its own 'Local Rules for Malvern Common,' including such items as 'The pond to the left hand side between the 4th and 5th Greens is out of bounds,' 'A ball shall not be considered unplayable merely from being covered with mud,' and 'A ball lying in horse or cow droppings or in a hoof or wheel track away from a hazard may be lifted, and it, or another one, dropped under penalty of one stroke, except on the Putting Greens, where there shall be no penalty.'

*

On with the golf lessons. Townshend's second chapter tackles the question of integrating 'inspiration' with the rest of a player's game, especially the flexing of the wrist. He advises solo practice in the garden, suggesting how to make a 'captive ball,' and in his references to 'experimental psychology' continues to encourage the golfer to think about his game as much as possible.

CHAPTER 2: BODY AND MIND

To make the idea of 'inspiration' fit in with the other ideas on the golfing swing already packed away in your mind is the next question. You take up a club in order to swing at a daisy with the whole of the fifteen maxims I have before quoted lying doggo in your subconscious self, each simply aching to attract your attention. As you swing, some one of them will have succeeded in pushing itself into the foreground of the mental view, while the others are half, or hardly half, perceived in the background. And right into the limelight in the foreground of this mental picture you now have to crowd another item, the deep inspiration I recommended. How are you to manage it?

This is a problem in experimental psychology (which is all the go nowadays) and by attacking it we raise ourselves to the dignity of philosophers. But philosophy is nothing if not scientific, so let us ensure that our psychological experiment is made scientifically. We must eliminate to begin with, so far as we can, all outside distracting influences. Therefore, I say, try your experiment quietly in solitude by yourself. Let me repeat, of all things don't begin to experiment when you are actually engaged in a match with an opponent. You will most likely lose your match, which matters little, and you will probably ruin your experiment, which to you may matter much. For the nervousness you will feel in trying it in a match, when you know that if you fail you will infallibly proceed to nag at yourself the whole of the rest of the round for having thrown the game away, is enough by itself to spoil any stroke. As you value your future golf, then, do not experiment like that. Try the new way of striking when the fate of the ball is a matter of no importance whatsoever. That is the true method of science.

Choose therefore a quiet part of the links where you will not be in anybody's way: choose also one where you are not likely to lose your ball. For if you are in a state of anxiety lest you should hit somebody else, or lest your ball should fly off into the rough and hide, your mind will be distracted. As you swing, you will be thinking of what may happen to the ball, and your eye which you are trying to keep on the spot where the ball lies will be instinctively fidgeting to follow its flight. To escape this temptation I advise you to experiment with captive balls. The plus man may scoff at them, saying that with a captive ball you can't tell whether you hook or slice. He is right enough there, of course, but then we are not out just now to contend with hooking and slicing; we are after something else. And that something else can be very successfully observed with a captive ball in your own garden.

You can easily buy a captive ball or make one for yourself. A golf-ball hampered by a yard of double string with a pair of champagne corks at the end can hardly be induced to fly fifty yards even by the strongest driver, while you as a weak brother may quite likely find forty to be your full limit. But if you haven't got forty yards of free range in your garden all you have to do is to tie on more corks. You can stop the strongest flier in ten yards if you only put on clogs enough.

Next we come to the question of teeing up. I cannot believe that even a high tee does a weak brother any harm, whatever its effect may be on the plus man, and I am sure that if you want to save the turf of your lawn from unsightly scars you will have to use a tee. This again can be bought in the market at a price anywhere from twopence to two shillings, and of these tees of the shop there are many varieties: or you may commandeer from the gardener or buy at the ironmonger's a foot or so of common rubber garden hose, an inch or seven-eighths of an inch in diameter, and cut it (with a wetted knife) into tees of any height you choose. I should recommend you to cut it into sizes of ¼, ½, ¾, and one inch in height. Join them in assorted pairs, with a bit of red rag tied between, to keep them from going off too far and to make them easy to find.

So now at last we are ready for action. Tee up a captive, home-made or bought, and take your club in hand. Stand back in order that you may try a preliminary swing at a daisy, watch your own mind as you strike. After you have struck ask yourself immediately what you remember having had in the foreground of your mental view. The inspiration was there of course: you were out for that: you can scarcely fail to remember how you first ex-spired as you soled your club, and then in-spired deeply while keeping the club-face close to the ball, how you continued to hold the breath in during the up-swing, and breathed it out as the stroke finished. There was no difficulty about that: the novelty of the idea of inspiration enabled you to keep your attention firmly fixed.

But how about the other fifteen points, which you had in your mental background, in the keeping of the unconscious self? What happened to them? Tax your memory sternly, demand whether it can recall any thing of any of them. Ask it first as to the beginning of the swing. Did the wrists start the club back? Did they take it up slow? Was the left wrist flexed so as to be hollow at the top? During that sequence of three motions, or rather three parts of one motion, you were primarily, no doubt, busy over the question of keeping the lungs full; but you must bully your memory to tell you something about those other three also. How much it will tell is bound to vary indefinitely with the individual who makes the experiment. Smith's memory may be able distinctly to recall the details of all three. Jones's may have no definite picture of any; all it contains may be a vague idea that the left wrist was bent out stiffly when at the top, and consequently the up swing was not given time enough to finish itself out and the down swing began a little too soon, with the result that the body came through before the arms.

Suppose yourself to be Jones, and suppose your memory to have retained thus much of the action. Swing again (waggle and ex-spire, sole and inspire) and mind, now, you flex that wrist right at the top. You strike. Round comes the club with a whish-h-h, and you are conscious not only that you did contrive to hold your breath but also that you did flex that wrist rightly. You managed to have both images in the foreground of your mind at once, so to speak, the tightly closed mouth and the flexed, hollowed wrist; you had to do a sort of mental squint, but both things were in the view.

Perhaps you did not manage it. In that case swing again and see if you can control your mental action better. Never mind the rest of the fifteen old maxims; concentrate on that last one only, the hollowing or flexing of the wrist at the top, not of course forgetting inspiration. I have set you really an easy task, for by the time you get to the top of the swing you have about done with the inspiring; the breath is ready to be exhaled, and the effort to hold it may be allowed to relax, while the effort to give that flex to the wrist continues.

Now then, address the solid ball itself and not the meek daisy this time. Sole your club. Swing. Let her go! Hurrah, you have managed it. You did flex the wrist without having forgotten to hold the breath. You have made an experiment in psychology, and your golf begins to be inspired.

Interlude 1893: 'Rather Sporting, I Think?'

Elgar's first year of Club membership, 1893, did not really get going until the autumn. Shortly after his election to the Worcestershire Club in March, the Elgars went to stay for a few days with Minnie Baker, who lived near to Hasfield, and there was a chance to work there with RBT again. As well, Elgar got in plenty of putting practice with friends in Malvern, playing on the communal lawn outside his little house in Malvern Link, 'Forli.' Alice joined in, and thought her standard 'very good.' Her husband's early choral work, 'The Black Knight,' was successfully premièred in April, and in August the pair left for a month's holiday in Germany, returning in time for the Worcester Three Choirs Festival. Afterwards, there was at last some time for consistent golf practice. Elgar now played regularly for the remainder of the year, sometimes with RBT, sometimes with Dyke Acland, sometimes with Hugh Blair, the assistant organist of Worcester cathedral, and sometimes with another friend Nevinson, a local architect. Since he had a teaching round that took him to Malvern Wells once a week, Elgar fitted in some golf at the nearby Club whenever he could, wearing outdoor clothes and long gaiters for convenience instead of formal teaching garb. But in those conventional days, the wearing of such clothing might be considered quite improper out of context. In later years the composer liked to relate how one day a Headmistress was waiting behind a rosebush to ambush him as he arrived. 'Good morning, Mr. Elgar,' she said. 'Rather sporting, I think?' The golfer, determined not to be put off his stroke, merely replied, '<u>Very</u> sporting!' and passed on. Another such arrival at The Mount School in Great Malvern caused great excitement among the pupils. 'The news got round quickly,' wrote the Headmistress, Miss Burley, ' and by the time he left a good many girls had found vantage points overlooking the drive. There was much discussion as to whether using a violin bow was any training for a golf-club . . .'

But other golfing battles were not so easily won that year. One day Alice recorded that he came home 'vesy dejected' after a game, and at the end of November he 'sprained his fumb' and had to stop playing for a whole month, which made him rather 'misy.' Not until Boxing Day was he able to go the Club for some practice, but the course was too full. So keen was Elgar to get some golf that he took the train to Stoke Prior near Bromsgrove, where his sister lived, to play there. Some photographs of Elgar playing golf were taken on that or another occasion at Stoke Prior; RBT took some photographs at Hasfield Court but only one seems to have survived.

Elgar practised for an hour and half at Stoke, but only succeeded in further straining his thumb so that when RBT came over to Malvern from Hasfield next day, the composer accompanied him to the Club but was unable to play. Not to be deterred, RBT played eighteen holes by himself and returned to Forli to enjoy stout and oysters with the Elgars before catching the train back to Hasfield from Malvern Link station.

*

Having made his points about 'inspiration' and the use of the wrists, Townshend now uses his third chapter to mark time with reminders about the importance of thoughtful concentration while practising, adding some good advice about the right attitude to failure: 'smile.' He invokes the names of two unlikely bedfellows in the course of his exhortations; Molière's Monsieur Jourdain, the rich bourgeois determined to become a properly educated gentleman, who is astounded to realise that he has talked in prose all his life, and James Braid, the tall Scot who was five times British Open Champion between 1901 and 1910. And he invokes too, the first of those classical references, elucidated in the Appendix.

Appassionato

CHAPTER 3: NO TRIFLING

Well, you have now had one shot if no more at inspired golf, and the next question for you is whether you care to go on with it. People do vary so very greatly with regard to matters of this sort; some folks are quite able to make up their minds in half a minute as to whether a thing is going to suit them, or the contrary; whereas others may take a month to think about it, and then they don't know. "If you hear me talk," as the Far West cowboys used to say when I was ranching out there fifty years ago, you will scarcely content yourself with giving inspiration so mean a test as only a bare half minute; you will try it, at the least, let us say, for half an hour. And be sure that you make that half hour's trial a fair one. Whether you choose to strike at a free ball on the links or at a captive in the garden give your mind wholly to the act of striking, and do it with 'intention' in the full philosophic sense of the word. Don't go worrying yourself about what may happen to the ball; leave that to take care of itself; concentrate absolutely on what you do in the striking.

There lies the essence of all practice that is to be of any real worth to you, concentration. Knocking a golf ball casually about may be good enough as a form of exercise in order to open your pores and limber up your muscles, but it won't help your golf much. To improve, you must bend your whole mind to the shot. Twenty shots struck with intention are of more value than two hundred which are only half meant. Give yourself time to think between them; twenty in half an hour will be quite enough. And use self-examination. Analyse after each stroke; think where it differed from the previous stroke; think of what you would wish to alter in the next. Don't beat your breast or use Western cowboy swears, if you top or foozle. Say to yourself plainly, "that happened because I broke some law," and then see if you can spot which law it was, and when and how you broke it. Tee up again, and try not to break the same law in the same way next time. Above all don't worry. Smile at your failures. Smile.

Remember that your practice should not go on too long. Such powers of attention as your mind may have are invaluable, but they are also easily overstrained. Look backwards and reflect on the days of your youth, when you were a boy at school; how long a single hour in form then seemed, how weary and inattentive your mind used to grow before the end. Yet then you only had Latin and Greek to wrestle with, or perhaps Euclid. Now you are up against golf, a very different proposition from trifling with Propria quae maribus or the Pons Asinorum. As I once heard a wise old clerical golfer exclaim with fervent emphasis, "Remember you can't trifle with golf!"

He was absolutely right, and therefore you cannot afford to trifle with this inspiration idea. No, give the cure I have ventured to suggest to you a fair show; don't give it only the dregs of your mind; let each inspired shot have the full benefit of every atom of will-power you can dispose of. If you do this faithfully you soon will be able to judge whether the cure is likely to suit your case or not.

Suppose it does not, then *cadit quaestio*. There is nothing more to say, and you may shut up these pages; it will be better for you to go on as you are. But if the inspiration tip shows signs of being a help, then don't hurry the cure. Don't start out to make a trial of it by going out at once to play in a match and insisting on sedulously inspiring before each shot. Of course you might do so and find it a help right from the start, but you might also find it tend to make you too self-conscious and so put you off. Go on and play your match by all means, golf is a game and what you are after is amusement, but don't insist to yourself while playing that you are going to inspire. If when you strike off you find that your breath is inclined to hold itself, as it were automatically, why let it do so, but don't worry over it. Don't go asking yourself every time did you or did you not inspire before that shot. On the contrary, try to play your game in your ordinary style as far as you conveniently can, letting all this new inspiration business slide.

But the next day – or better still the same day, after you have finished your game and have had tea and rested - then take out a club and ball and give your inspired golf a few minutes trial, just enough to be interesting but not to make you feel stale. Do this daily for a week, and then go out and play a match in which at every tee, and if you like, before every shot through the green, and before every putt, you practise this new scheme of inspiration. A week will have given you time to adjust yourself to the new dodge mentally and bodily, and you now are not likely to find that it makes you produce anything worse than the weak brother's usual performance with which you are only too painfully familiar. Even if you do fall below your own humble par, you may ask yourself whether this is not simply due to nervousness caused by the novelty, and try whether after playing a few more matches this first nervousness will not disappear. If you still find yourself losing games steadily when you know that you ought not, then you will at last have a fair right to say, "Inspiration for me is a fraud."

Here let me make you a present of one suggestion. It is just possible that there was no need for you to inspire, because you had already been practising it unconsciously, just as Molière's *bourgeois gentilhomme* had talked prose all his life without knowing it. There is such a thing as a habit changing itself automatically, and this may have been the case with you. Think over the past. Was there ever a time when you noticed a sudden improvement in your game? Possibly at that very time you did, quite spontaneously, adopt my remedy. James Braid has told us that from being only a moderate driver (moderate in his class, that is,) he suddenly became a long one without knowing why. Can it have been due to an unconscious alteration in his way of breathing? If so he must be the very Monsieur Jourdain of golf.

Well, we may leave that matter to settle itself; each of us must analyse his own inner consciousness in his own way. But let us suppose that after a week's private practice you try inspiration in a match and find that you seem to be the better for it rather than the worse. Then go ahead, but continue practising your new method in private as well as in matches.

And do not forget that if Monsieur Jourdain's prose was unconsciously acquired the rest of the desired accomplishments were attained by purposeful application. The *bon bourgeois* did not trifle over the education of a *gentilhomme,* but carefully concentrated himself on what might seem the most trivial of details. You should imitate him on this point no less carefully, and whether you are thinking of inspiration, or wrist work, or follow through, or any other maxim, at the very instant of the act you must focus your whole mind on it, and, as the writer of Proverbs has it, 'Do it with thy might.' There is to be no trifling with golf.

Interlude 1894: Six Lost Balls

The new year saw a recovery from the thumb problem, and further investment in suitable clothing with the purchase of what Alice called a 'golf Ulster;' January weather is not always conducive but the new coat enabled Elgar to play at the Club on ten occasions during the month, including a game with the Reverend T. Littleton Wheeler, Secretary of the Worcester Three Choirs Festival Committee, another important contact for the ambitious composer. Wheeler was sympathetic. Some years earlier, he had sent Elgar an official letter of appreciation from the Committee in recognition of the 'Froissart' Overture, endorsing it personally with his own 'hearty concurrence.' And at Hasfield Elgar played in a foursome (which he always liked to call 'a fearsome') against no less a distinguished-sounding figure than Sir Capel Wolsely. The two men played again a couple of days later, and it might seem that Sir Capel was as much a newcomer to the royal and ancient game as Elgar, for Alice wrote that between them they 'lost about 6 balls.'

Despite a short period of illness at the end of January, Elgar was able to send off his partsong 'O Happy Eyes' to the publishers as well as resume his teaching. At the beginning of April the Townshends descended on Malvern Wells for a couple of weeks, staying nearby; perhaps RBT was determined to master the Club course with all its vagaries. Elgar played with his tutor as frequently as he could that month, eager to improve his game; on one occasion, Alice noted, they played all day, with a break for a crab lunch at the Club House. In the middle of it all there was a decided musical success for Elgar, the first performance at Worcester cathedral of a ceremonial piece specially requested by Hugh Blair to mark the visit of the Duke of York, later King George V, to the City. The music was written for strings, brass, timpani and organ, and was called 'Sursum Corda' – 'Lift up your Hearts.' The instrumental colouring of the music was impressive but for the time being no publisher was interested in it.

Elgar's appetite for the game of games was evidently now thoroughly whetted, and at the beginning of May he and Alice went on a golfing holiday to Littlehampton, with its seaside links course. They stayed at 44, South Terrace, a house still to be found, but the weather was windy, cold and 'misy' and not a great deal of golf was possible. Instead the pair enjoyed some sightseeing in Chichester, Arundel, and Brighton before breaking their return journey at Oxford to see the Townshends. RBT took Elgar to see his local course, but heavy rain spoilt any plans for a game.

Once back in Malvern, Elgar made up for lost time by playing on six days in succession, and he continued playing as much as he could for the rest of 1894. In fact, he never again played more golf than he did that year, for his wife's diary mentions some 87 games altogether. Several times he was at the Club all day again, playing familiar opponents – Littleton-Wheeler, Sir Capel, Dyke Acland. But this year the names of some new golfing partners appear in Alice's diary, including those of Basil Nevinson, the cello-playing, bug-hunting brother of the Malvern architect, and Richard Penrose Arnold, son of the famous poet and critic, who after a somewhat erratic earlier career – he had been sent down twice from Balliol because of his drinking and gambling - settled to the life of a factory inspector. Both men would be important for their fellow-golfer's future music. Richard Arnold lived in Worcester, and was no doubt one of those whose golfing at Malvern Wells was made more convenient by the flexibility of the railway company over their timetables. He was an *intuitive music-lover who made sure to attend a performance of Elgar's early Cantata, 'The Black Knight' conducted by Hugh Blair at Hereford on Friday 10th November. 'I think it was <u>splendid</u>,' he wrote next day, and went on to discuss the orchestration and performance in a highly appreciative way. The letter did not neglect other important matters, however. 'Are we going to play golf on Tuesday afternoon next?' it concluded. Sure enough the two men enjoyed a round that day, and repaired to Forli, to take tea with Alice Elgar and Arnold's wife Ella. '<u>Very</u> nice time,' wrote the composer's wife, who always decidedly took to anyone who showed genuine enthusiasm for her husband's music.*

Elgar remained keen to improve his game, playing in a competition that month despite coming home 'wet through,' according to Alice. The previous month she had noted that he came home from the Club 'misy from not playing well.' He 'practised drives' at Hasfield and reaped some reward when, on 22nd November, appropriately enough perhaps St. Cecilia's Day, he managed each of the 10th, 11th and 12th holes in 4. He was playing against F. A. Horn, Chairman of the Green Committee, 'old Horn,' as Elgar seems to have called him. Perhaps it was his brother, C. A. Horn, known to all as 'Cape Horn' whose name later appears in the Club records as having twice holed out in 73, and who achieved a 74, equalling the record, for the Club's Monthly Competition Medal in 1908.

*

Never short of an imaginative, not to say unusual approach to teaching, Townshend now draws for his fourth chapter on a vivid memory of his days in New Mexico, when he saw a religious fanatic flagellating his back using a two-handed scourge over the shoulder. It seemed a perfect example of how to encourage the golfer to 'follow through' properly, bringing the club well down the back after the stroke.

Practical and down-to-earth as ever, Townshend was not above recommending his pupil to make a notice summarising his three major points so far - inspiration, wrists and follow-through - and put it where it could be seen from the tee.

CHAPTER 4: PLAYING PENITENTE

We may suppose now that the idea of inspired golf has become tolerably familiar to your mind, and that you no longer need to keep the limelight on it so strongly while you address the ball. The next step in our course of experimental psychology is to see just how large a variety of the older ideas stowed away in our subconscious self we can combine with the act of inspiration at the moment of striking. Variety, that's what we need to keep us from being bored; and did not Voltaire, the great philosopher, say of education, "Every method is good except the one that bores you." The same thought occurred to Lin McLean, the cowboy hero of Owen Wister's cleverest story, when he suddenly determined to quit cow-punching, and remarked to the startled ranch foreman who wanted to know why, "What's the matter with some variety?"

Here, then, is the particular variety that I would next offer you. Tee up, as before, and I don't care a jot whether you tee a free ball on the links or a captive in the garden; and begin operations once again with the usual preliminary swing. You have already got the habit of inspiration at the beginning of the stroke as well as of using the wrists properly, even at the risk of giving yourself a mental squint by the attempt to keep both points steadily in view at the same time. Now I propose to introduce a third object into the foreground of your mental view, namely the posture at the finish. Consider the many fine finishes you have seen when watching golfers strike off, and the many pictures you have admired in books and newspapers which have been taken of them in the act. What is it that has struck you the most? I suppose the way in which the arms and hands have come out away from the body in front and very often have swung clean round to the left till the club has finished right down behind the back. Not all the fine players bring the club so far round, but all, I think without exception, get the hands away so that the club comes right through. Tell yourself that you will do the same as you address your daisy for the preliminary swing. As before, you can put down a gun-wad or a scrap of paper if you happen to be short of daisies.

Swing, then, remembering both to inspire and to flex the wrist, and also to insist on the club coming through. Perhaps you find that the club seems to wish to pull itself up short before the finish is completed. If so, don't let it do so; shove it on; keep it moving, aye, till it fairly hits you in the small of the back. Hitting yourself in the small of the back may be an exaggeration of the ideal follow-through, but then it pays to exaggerate sometimes. My name for this exaggeration finish down the back is playing the Penitente.

Let me tell you why. On a certain day in Lent, now alas! over forty years ago, I rode into a very remote village of what was then the very remote Territory of New Mexico. I saw the people (many of whom I knew) standing about in groups apparently occupied in watching some performance, and then in their midst I caught sight of a mysterious white object, moving about very queerly and acting in a way that I could not make out or understand. I rode closer, and what I beheld was this. A human being, stripped naked save for a pair of loose white drawers, and also for a loose white cotton muffler that entirely swathed its head, was dragging itself about with long half-kneeling steps in a bent posture. Its two hands grasped a soap-weed scourge, and the scourge was red, and the bare back was red, and there were red stains on the white cotton drawers down below. At each dragging step the creature raised the hands that held the bloody scourge and brought it sharply over the shoulder so that it came with a whish-h-h down the back. This ghastly self-torturer was one of a band of Penitentes or flagellants, who publicly flogged themselves every year in Lent, and I was destined to learn a good deal more about the horrid business and the people who took part in it; but that is a long story which I have partially told elsewhere.

However, I have never forgotten the first sight of that awful Penitente slashing himself down the back; and every time on the links that I indulge in a preliminary swing with an exaggerated follow-through his figure rises before my memory. And if I want to remind myself of the importance of bringing the club right through and well down the back I look back upon that strange scene under the torrid New Mexican sun and bid myself, "Play Penitente."

Those poor benighted self-torturers slashed their backs as a penitential atonement for their sins. Come on, then, weak brother, and do your share of penance to atone for your golfing sins of the past. It is up to you now, as we used to say out west, to be a Penitente. Fix your eye on that meek daisy, inspire, swing, strike, and make that club whistle through till it hits you where the Penitente hit himself. Now address the teed ball, fill your lungs again, hit it for all you're worth, and fetch that club through. Did you fail to get it through with the ball, where you had succeeded with the daisy? That very likely was because the shock of the collision with the ball checked the club. Never mind. Tee up another, take a full breath once more, and strike off again. You may not succeed the second or even the third time, but persevere, and you will do so eventually and will get off a shot in which, after smiting not the empty air but the solid ball, you find that you have succeeded in bringing the club quite through until it finished down across your back.

Now at once apply the self-examination process. Did you keep in mind the inspiration and the right use of wrists in the up-swing as well as the third idea of following-through at the finish? Probably you were all right with the inspiration, for that came at the very beginning, but possibly you slurred the wrist action. Anyhow you had better swing again and again till you manage to keep all three points in your mind together and slur none. If you like to avail yourself of a small material aid to this, write on a piece of paper in large letters

INSPIRE
USE WRISTS
FOLLOW THROUGH

And stick it up on an impromptu stand right opposite your tee, just where on many links the stick up a notice "REPLACE THE DIVOT." Look at it before you begin the swing and fix your attention firmly on it. You will find the effort to keep this triple bill in mind rather fatiguing, but go on doing it steadily for several shots. Take a rest, lest you grow stale, and do something else for a few minutes. Then begin again, and repeat the process, always laying the chief emphasis on the third of the trio, the last item of your mental programme. Concentrate entirely upon that, upon the determined follow-through. Let your club hit you hard on the back every time. You know you deserve it for your past sins. At all costs make yourself play the Penitente.

Interlude 1895: Geese, Cucumbers, Broccoli and Children

1895 was an important stage for Elgar in his development as a composer and in the gradual widening of his reputation; he produced his choral songs 'From the Bavarian Highlands,' a large Sonata for Organ for his golfing friend Hugh Blair, and began his Cantata, 'Scenes from the Saga of King Olaf.' In December the Worcester Committee agreed to accept another choral work, 'Lux Christi,' for the Festival the following year. Perhaps those rounds at the Club with Littleton-Wheeler bore some fruit with this commission. Elgar had written to him the previous month suggesting the idea, and received in return a promise to bring the matter to the attention of something he called 'the Committee.' And he continued, 'I am glad to hear you have something which you can offer us, and shall be very interested in hearing more about it. Can you play Golf on Friday?' The golf was duly played, Littleton-Wheeler's curiosity about the work was no doubt satisfied and barely three weeks later he was able to write to the composer that he was 'very pleased to tell you that the Music Subcommittee have agreed to recommend the Executive Committee to accept your new work;' certainly the Festival Secretary was in the best position to know his way through such a maze of committees.

With such an amount of work on his hands, Elgar played less golf this year, but not markedly so, continuing to fit the game into his teaching round as much as possible and totting up about sixty-five matches in all. January snow found him undeterred, and June saw him playing in a Club competition. Perhaps it was one of those days when, in Wodehouse's words, 'all nature shouted "Fore!"' because Alice recorded that although her husband 'did not win,' he came home 'vesy cheerful.'

Win or lose, Elgar had his own philosophy of golf, which he once summed up in a typed memorandum, perhaps in response to a request from a newspaper. 'Outdoor exercise is absolutely essential to life,' he began, and continued, 'Golf, call it a game, a sport or what you will, no-one can define golf, is the best form of exercise for writing-men, as it involves no risk of accident, is always ready without waiting for a "side," or a clear court as ie Lawn-tennis &c.' As a 'writing-man' himself Elgar was in an excellent position to praise golf for its ready availability, and we have seen how easily he fitted the game into his timetable. To be able to get out of the house and enjoy some activity in the fresh air was always one of his priorities, for he prided himself on not being the kind of composer who sat behind a desk scratching his head for inspiration. (That word again!) Rather he thought that 'music is in the air all around you,' and you took as much of it as you wanted. So it is likely that, more and more, golf on Peachfield Common, with its close views of the Malvern Hills and their endlessly varying skyscapes, was becoming a stimulus for Elgar to think music, rather than being a mere pastime.

The composer was less than accurate, however, in defining golf as a game with no risk of accident, at any rate as far as the very open position of the Worcestershire Club was concerned. Various ladies in passing carriages were struck by golf balls on various occasions, and a neighbouring cottager was awarded ten shillings in compensation for the death of two geese; he was told that no further claims would be considered without the production of the deceased. Another neighbour demanded restitution to the extent of £1.9.0 in the matter of damage to cucumbers, broccoli and his children. But let us rest assured that these incidents happened before the election of Mr Edward Elgar to the Club.

Sometime towards the middle of October he again played with Richard Penrose Arnold, and again invited him home to tea, and played him some of the 'King Olaf' music. Arnold was hugely impressed, and went home so full of his enthusiasm that his wife immediately wrote to Alice, 'Dick has come home perfectly <u>possessed</u> by Mr Elgar & his wonderful cleverness (that is hardly the word) – He says Schumann was a babe compared to him, & can think & talk of <u>nothing</u> else – I need not say he adored his afternoon.' Such support - and unquestioned social acceptance - from a cultured fellow-golfer, and a son of one of Victorian England's most distinguished literary figures to boot, must have been greatly welcome.

*

Townshend, who has so far like a good pedagogue taken things one step at a time, with plenty of scope for revision, goes on to deal with two points at once in the next chapter; the twist of the body, and the position of the feet, especially the left foot, at the finish of the stroke. Once again he tries a little 'experimental psychology' in suggesting that an approach exactly opposite to the one required could be a good way of learning. And once again he finds a memorable phrase to help the learner remember, a phrase he had heard from a cowboy and which evidently became something of a favourite, 'vim, vinegar and vitriol.'

Land of Hope and Glory

CHAPTER FIVE : VIM, VINEGAR AND VITRIOL

Suppose we proceed to try yet another little variety. By this time we may assume that a deep inspiration before each shot is taken for granted. The action should already have become part of the unconscious self so far as to be a sort of automatic process that we go through every time we address the ball. And perhaps the unconscious self will also be kind enough to take charge of the other two points to both of which we have been attending or trying to attend at one and the same time, namely, the use of the wrists in the up-swing and the prolonged follow-through at the finish; we have been keeping the limelight on these two; now we will put them back into the middle distance of the mental view and bring up another pair of fresh points into the foreground. As in the former case it will be convenient if the two fresh points come, not just exactly together in the stroke, but one later than the other. The first point I will take is the twist of the body: this goes on right through the up-swing while the wrists (and arms) are taking the club up. Of course you will carefully remind yourself to inspire as you address the ball, but be careful also not to think too much about it: concentrate your mind resolutely, and focus it on the body-twist; neither should you think too much about the wrist-work; let your wrists, as it were, take the club up of themselves (slowly) while the active part of your brain is busy seeing to it that your left hip turns clear through a right-angle till it comes opposite the ball. This is partly because such an almost acrobatic twisting of the bodily frame is a movement quite unusual, not to say unnatural, and partly because when you mean to strike, your will is wound up hard for action and gets impatient to be done with the necessary slowness of the body-twist; what the wound-up will craves for is to loose off instanter in the swift strong blow. Keep a tight rein on the will, then; check the impulse to a premature delivery of the blow, ever the most fatal of errors; go on twisting the hip till you know it has come round opposite the ball; incidentally this will give time for the wrists to carry the club well up and to flex themselves, with the left bent in under properly, at the top of the swing; never mind even if there should be a very perceptible moment's pause at the top. True the plus men seem to swing like lightning, with no pause anywhere; but then, my friend, you and I are not plus men, very far from it; their counsels of perfection are not for us; we may permit ourselves to pause a moment at the top of the swing, or do anything else that may save us from hurrying into the error of plunging into the down-swing prematurely.

Look at your daisy, then, and swing at it, keeping the body-twist in the limelight of the mental view, pause momentarily at the top, and then smite that daisy, as I once heard a Far West cowboy say, with vim, vinegar and vitriol. Slaughter the daisy thus a few times till you feel sure of yourself, and then have a go at the teed ball. After twisting the body so much round you will probably find yourself less likely than usual to hit the ball with the exact middle of the club-face, but if and when you do succeed in doing so, the ball will surely fly further than it ever was wont to do for you in the past.

Here, then, is the first of the two fresh points we are trying to keep an eye on, the right-angled twist of the body. The second of them shall be a point coming later in the swing, namely the position of the feet and especially the left foot at the finish. In your last few shots the odds are that if you have happened to notice your position at the finish you will have observed that your feet have moved away from the original stance. This may be an old trouble with you, and you may have long known how you are given to swing yourself off your stance; but you are certainly more likely to find that you have done it when you got in all that extra body work in those last shots. Now go over your recollections again of how a fine golfer shapes at the finish, recalling details of his attitude either from what you have yourself observed or from pictures. When we looked at his finish before, the point to which we directed our attention was the way he got his hands away; turn your eyes now not to his hands but to his feet. Is not his left foot set firmly on the ground, with the heel well down and the weight inclining to lean on the outside of the foot? Indeed so strongly is this particular point marked in some of the best photographs that they almost recall the idea of a skater doing the outside edge and striking out on the left foot. No doubt you may occasionally see a fine driver swing with such abandon that the exuberance of his finish carries him right off his feet, but even he only exceeds in this manner at a certain risk, and you may be very sure that his left foot is never raised before the ball has left the face of the club, whatever he does with it after.

For an experiment, go to the opposite extreme, and see if you can compel yourself to do a shot with the maximum of immobility. Address your daisy, and say to yourself, "Flatfooted! Heels and toes both down!" and take a full swing so. You will find it very hard or even impossible either to get the right-angled body-twist without raising the left heel, or to follow well through and get the club away till it comes round down the back without having raised the right; but never mind that; this is only an experiment, and you had better neglect all other matters for the present so long as you keep both feet firm and flat on the ground the whole time. After a few preliminary trials at the daisy, just to assure yourself that it really is possible to strike without raising either foot at all, tee up a ball and strike it in the same manner. If you have happened to strike it fair you will be quite surprised to see how well it travels in spite of the rather cramped swing, and you will perhaps note that your shoulders at the finish came into a tolerably correct attitude. This will help you to realize that it is unnecessary to swing yourself off your feet, and that a full free swing that leaves you with the left foot firmly planted at the finish is likely to give the best possible results. So after a few of these flat-footed swings, you may allow first one and then both heels to rise in turn and see if you can contrive to let yourself go in a freer swing while firmly determined on keeping your stance. If you have been in the habit of falling off it this will not be an easy task; but you have got to do it, and remember that the more vigour you put into the shot the harder you will find it to remain firm on your feet at the finish. Play a short mashie approach, and it is easy enough to keep the feet firm, but it is quite another thing when you put every ounce of force you have into a full drive. For if you are really to make it go, weak, half-hearted hitting is no good, and the half-hearted blow itself is surely a symptom of acedia creeping on. Don't surrender to it, then. To get distance you must put in the last ounce and you have got to hit that ball as the Western cowboy put it, with vim, vinegar and vitriol.

Interlude 1896: Jones, "Hookham," Toppin, Paterson and "Horn"

Very often during these years Elgar seems to have referred to his golfing partners with a typically Victorian mix of formality and schoolboy familiarity. In those days even friends were very often known to each other merely by surname. A closer friendship might be demonstrated not by a Christian name, but by the use of initials. Thus the music-loving Richard Arnold, with whom Elgar was continuing to play golf regularly, sometimes became 'RPA' in Alice's diary.

Non-musical golfing partners were usually referred to initially at any rate just as 'Mr' by Alice. With the development of some degree of friendship, the surname alone might be used, and a final stage might be the suggestion of some friendly leg-pulling with the surname framed in speechmarks. "Horn" and a certain "Hookham" were subjected to this treatment, and so were various other Elgarian golfers, some of them Club officers and distinguished players. F. A. Horn would be Captain of the Club for 1897 and his greenkeeping was such that 'Golf Annual' sang his praises, writing 'The putting greens are carefully looked after and run very keen.' Dyke Acland himself had won the Club's Easter Challenge Prize in 1889, a silver salver. Among the composer's other golfing partners were a certain Paterson, one-time Club Secretary, (who also won the Easter Challenge one year as well as the 1898 Autumn Cup), one Toppin, Club Captain for that year and a cricket coach at Malvern College, and G. A. Jones, Captain in 1897.

Many of the golfing feats of these heroes of past days have been preserved in the Club Record Book, instituted in 1883. For example, it is recorded that on November 20th, 1890, Paterson did the fifth and sixth holes in 2 each. (The following year a Mr H. Buck, otherwise apparently unknown to Elgarian and golfing history, took 26 when playing the first hole on the upper course). In 1893, we are told, G. A. Jones when playing with "Horn," drove into the railway at the 10th hole. He teed up again, drove through one hedge and over another, and holed out in 4. And Toppin's March 1896 round of 71, including a two, three threes and nine fours was thought well worthy of mention, achieved on a course where because of its difficulties, anything between 70 and 80 was considered a highly meritorious score; Jones himself went round in 72 the same year.

Elgar's scores – his golfing ones, that is – seem generally to have been a well-kept secret, although his hour would come, as will be seen. His musical ones progressed well that year, with 'Lux Christi' premièred at Worcester in September, and 'King Olaf' at Hanley in October. The work involved meant a little less golf in the summer and autumn, but when he was free Elgar returned to the Club with a vengeance, playing frequently throughout December, braving another snowstorm on the 17th and squeezing some rounds in on both Christmas Eve and Boxing Day.

*

Townshend's thoroughly up-to-date mind leads him to suggest in the next chapter that the study of a film of the swing would be an excellent way of learning by one's mistakes. Realising the difficulty and expense of arranging such an 'action replay' for most people, he ingeniously suggests that the aid of the sun be invoked instead. If the player stand with his back to the sun, much can be learnt from the shadow, especially in relation to the movement of the head.

But he tends to dismiss all artificial aids and exercises in approaching the question of the intensification of the grip during the downswing. Here, once again, it is a matter of mental attitude and practice, and the long-suffering daisy comes in for some further punishment as a result.

Pipe dream

CHAPTER SIX : INTENSIFICATION

There is one extra-special petition beyond all other that every golfer must have often felt inclined to offer up:

O wad some Power the giftie gie us
To see oursel's as ithers see us!

Robert Burns may not have been a golfer, but he saw deep into the soul of man, and he knew – none better – how hard it is to get outside ourselves. This indeed has been the most real of the difficulties we have had to contend with, even though inspiration, the first point that we considered, hardly requires an external view. Your own internal sensations can tell you all about drawing the air into your lungs and holding it there, and you know just what you are doing without the aid of the eye. But when it comes to such a matter as the body being twisted through a right-angle or the wrists being properly bent at the top of the swing an outside view would be a real convenience.

The best way undoubtedly to get such a view would be to have a cinematograph film taken showing you in the act of swinging; you could then study the moving picture of yourself over and over, and spot your faults at your leisure; this might, however, cost more money than you care to spend. Let us see if we can find a less expensive substitute.

The simplest method of all is to call in the aid of the sun, not by the roundabout plan of getting yourself photographed on a film, but directly. On a sunshiny day, then, take your stand with your back to the sun, club in hand, and watch the tell-tale shadow of yourself. It will tell you if you rocked sideways on your stance, if you got your hands away, if you came well on to the left leg at the finish. One thing especially you can note accurately by this means, how much your head moves during the shot. Put a mark where the middle of your shadow's head comes, at the moment when you are addressing the ball; swing, and see where the shadow of the head has got to afterwards. I have tried this experiment with one of the finest golfers alive, one whose style experts have frequently singled out for praise, and I find that when he has the sun right at his back the shadow of his head at the finish is a good six inches more to the left than it was when he was addressing the ball. The shadow of the head does not move away from the mark during the up-swing, nor during the down-swing before the ball is hit, but afterwards it does move those few inches to the left, as also does the shadow of the body as well. I take this to be evidence that the fine golfer in question finishes with the weight of his body transferred to a considerable extent to the left foot, and this accords exactly with the impression left by the numerous pictures illustrating the way in which an ideal finish shows the left foot firmly planted and supporting the body. In ascertaining how far your own swing fulfils these desirable conditions you can have no better ally than the sun.

Take in the next place another most essential point, that of the firmness of the grip, and ask yourself, "Do you intensify in the down-swing?"

Neither your own eye nor some friendly instructor's eye can tell you anything whatever about that; it is purely a matter of internal self-observation. Swing at a daisy, and note the grip of either hand. What is your rule with regard to it? According to the best advice you should take firm hold with your left hand in order to start the club up with the wrist, and you are to keep that hold till the club gets to the top. The right hand must grip loosely in order to allow the club to turn as it goes up. To clench the club tightly with both hands inevitably produces a stiff cramped swing that would not do at all. But if you go on to perform the down-swing with this same loose grip the blow is likely to be both feeble and inaccurate. As the club descends the grip of both hands should tighten so that at the moment of impact the club is held as firmly as possible. The force of the blow delivered by the whole of your bodily frame has to be transferred to the club by the hands and then by the club to the ball. Supposing, then, that the hands holding the club are slack they cannot but fail efficiently to transmit the force of the body to the ball, and the resulting blow will be feeble.

If on consideration you come to the conclusion that your grip is weak you may try to strengthen it if you like by various gymnastic exercises, such as by squeezing balls, using dumbbells, and so forth, or even by simply clenching your hands tightly at intervals during the day whenever your memory reminds you to do so. This sort of thing is ineffably tedious, but there is no doubt you can thus strengthen your grip very considerably if you will be at the pains.

Do not forget, moreover, to look at the grips of your clubs occasionally; the place where the fingers come is apt to get polished and wants to be roughened again with a few touches of the file. Some men use pitch to help them keep tight hold of the club, and presumably they find it to their advantage. If you try this do it cautiously, for if you are thin-skinned a grip with too much pitch on it – too much for you, that is – would be quite liable to skin your hands. In all such matters, of course, common sense is above all necessary. There is no need to play the fool and say, "Happy thought! try pitch," and go out to play in a competition after putting a lot of adhesive stick-stuff on your clubs for the first time in your golfing life. The right place for a man who acted like that would be the golf-course attached to an idiot asylum.

I believe some men have experimented with oval and polygonal grips, but the innovation can hardly be said to have become popular. Possibly it may suit a few people. All one can say about it is to repeat the old jest, "For those who like this sort of thing, this is the sort of thing they would like." Similarly rubber grips seem to suit some golfers better than leather. And similarly one can only say, "Chacun son goût."

To return to this question of intensifying: the little dodges and appliances above mentioned may or may not be of some use; they can hardly make much difference; the all important thing is your own will-power. Fix your mind on taking the club up with a firm (but not a desperate) grip; then, as it descends in the down-swing, tighten your fingers on it for all you are worth. Nothing, inspiration only excepted, will do your blow so much good as this intensification of the grip at the psychological moment. It must take place in what is only a fraction of a second, and it must take place in the proper fraction of a second. Do it before the down-swing begins, and you cramp yourself; do it after the club has hit the ball, and it is a mere futility. There is only one proper fraction of a second in each case, and that comes during the first half of the down-swing. See if you can stab your will broad awake to put "vim, vinegar and vitriol" into that proper fraction. I have no objection to offer to the gymnastics, or the hand-grip exercises, or to taking up carpentering as a finger exercise, and all the rest of it; but these things are mere aids: what is vital at the critical quarter-second is the power of the will. Intensify.

'Eye on the ball' – Elgar inspires at Hasfield Court

Bernard Keeling, RBT's great-nephew, astride his wooden horse

Elgar's golfing friends . . . F. A. Horn, Chairman of the Green Committee, with the Club's Professional, G. H. Cawsey, apparently summoned from behind the bar . . .

. . . G. D. Carr, Club Secretary for many years

... and W. Paterson, Club Secretary 1900

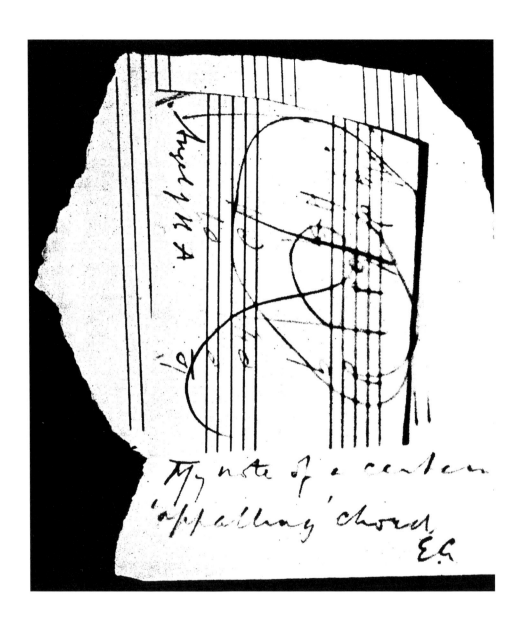

'Made probably on the golf links' – music for *The Dream of Gerontius*

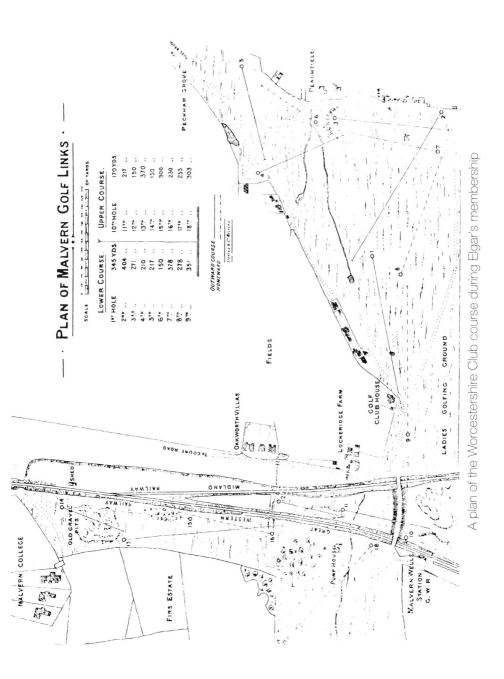

· PLAN OF MALVERN GOLF LINKS ·

SCALE

LOWER COURSE.		UPPER COURSE.	
1ST HOLE	170 YDS.	10TH HOLE	217
2ND ··	404	11TH ··	217
3RD ··	271	12TH ··	150
4TH ··	210	13TH ··	370
5TH ··	217	14TH ··	150
6TH ··	150	15TH ··	300
7TH ··	378	16TH ··	230
8TH ··	278	17TH ··	255
9TH ··	351	18TH ··	303

OUTWARD COURSE ____
HOMEWARD

A plan of the Worcestershire Club course during Elgar's membership

41

Off to the Links – Elgar and plus-fours at 'Craeg Lea,' 1903

The composer putting, with Carice poised to remove the flag

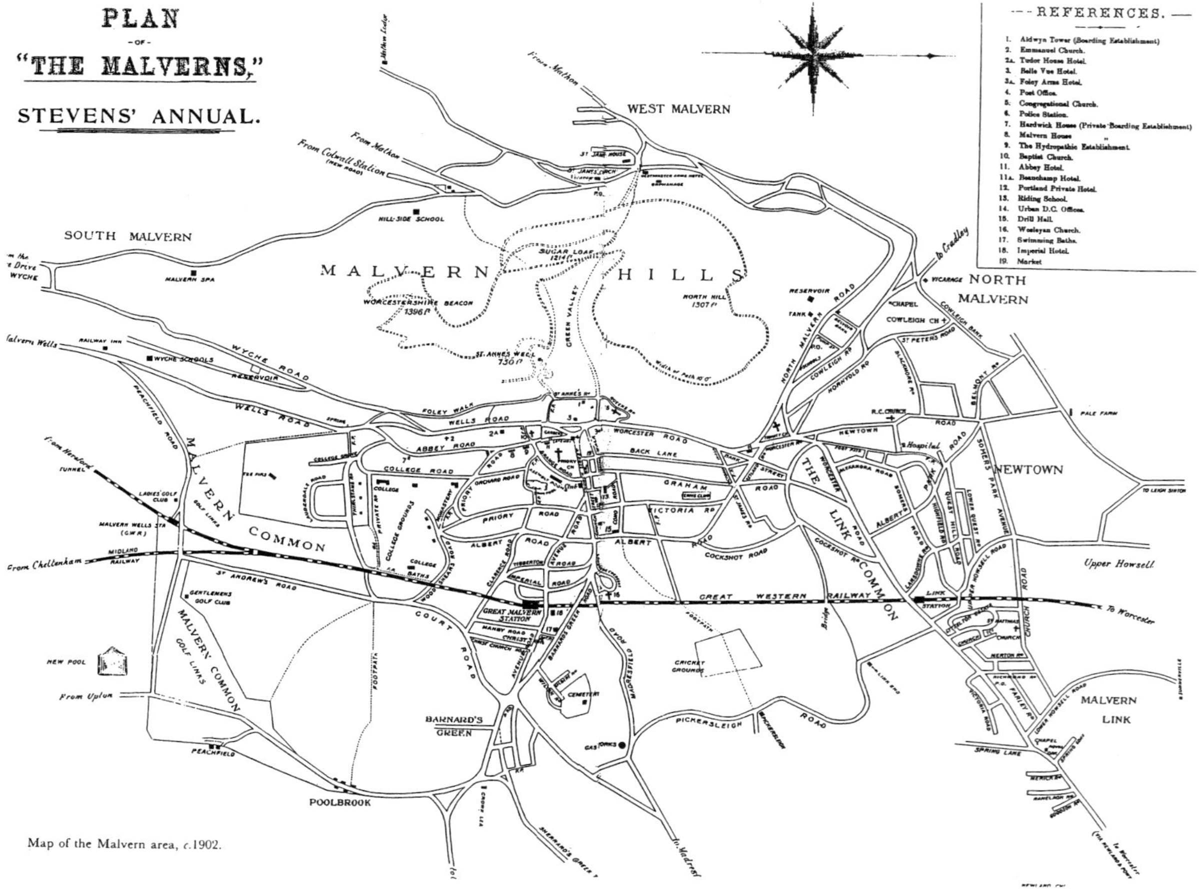

PLAN
-OF-
"THE MALVERNS,"
STEVENS' ANNUAL.

Map of the Malvern area, c.1902.

The route to the Links? – a street map of Malvern, c.1902

The WGC Club House, with caddies in attendance

A drive at the ninth

A three-ball match at the tenth

The thirteenth tee – and railway lines

Paterson at the fourteenth, with Malvern College in the background

A drive at the fifteenth

Amaryllis in the Garden? A sketch from the Norbury papers

The Ladies' Club House

Interlude 1897-98: A New Driver and 'Martial Tum Tum.'

With gradually growing fame and continuing demands on his time, Elgar seems never to have played less golf than during these years, only managing about forty visits to the Club over the whole two-year period. He composed his 'Imperial March' and 'Chanson de Nuit,' a Te Deum and Benedictus for the Hereford Festival, 'The Banner of St. George,' a commission from his publishers with Queen Victoria's approaching Jubilee in mind, and his largest work yet, 'Caractacus,' a cantata for four soloists, chorus and orchestra based on the legend of the Briton King's last stand against the Romans at the hill at the southern end of the range known as the British Camp. And it was arranged that he would become conductor of the Worcestershire Philharmonic Society, a body set up specially for him and in which he took a keen interest, spending much time in planning and supervising the details of the programmes.

Small wonder then that in 1898, the year of 'Caractacus,' he played golf just ten times, and sometimes he would catch the train from Malvern Link Station to the Wells, to save the time spent walking to the Club. The distance was said to be nearly five miles from the Link station to the course, as players unfamiliar with the area discovered when alighting there in the perfectly understandable expectation that a station with the word 'link' in its title might be adjacent to the greens. Elgar presumably took a 'short cut' when walking from his house in Alexandra Road to the Club, going along Graham Road, passing the house of his musical friends the Fittons, crossing Church Street, past the Assembly Rooms, along College Road to Malvern Common and so down and over the railway bridge to the Club. Even for an accustomed walker, as Elgar and indeed many people were in those days, it would have been a fair step with the return journey as well. And in between there would have been the expenditure of the considerable amount of energy required to play the game itself. It was all surely sufficient to get the adrenalin flowing, and as Elgar wrote in his typed memorandum of golf philosophy, the benefits derived would be a 'beneficent temper, or, I would rather say, a desire to possess the lastnamed.' It might well be the kind of mood which encouraged creative thinking.

The previous year, 1897, he had taken another golfing holiday with Alice, this time at Bournemouth. It seemed a more successful venture than the Littlehampton expedition, the weather proving conducive this time. Elgar managed four rounds in between walks to Canford Cliffs and Poole Harbour, and celebrated by acquiring a new driver.

Back at the Worcestershire Club, Richard Arnold continued a regular partner. He was always generous in his support of Elgar's music, and Dyke Acland too was continuing to prove a stalwart friend. When the Worcester Festival Choral Society met for the first rehearsal of 'King Olaf' under Hugh Blair, for example, there was a poor response. Blair had the reputation of being fond of the bottle - it was shortly found expedient for him to leave his post - and some of the choir looked down on the music as being that of the son of a local tradesman and piano-tuner. Acland seems to have intervened on the spot to give some of the singers a piece of his mind, and Elgar wrote him a letter of thanks. 'I was quite determined that the Prophet should be honoured in his own Country,' replied his fellow-golfer, '& also that the longsuffering & patient drill sergeant should receive a few thanks & indeed nothing more. I really believe that those Worcester amateurs believe that they are giving you a great treat by attending the practices ...'

And he went on to suggest an idea for a work based on St. Augustine, evoking a world of ancient Britons and Romans, Druids, woods, battle-axes, mistletoe, and 'martial tum tum.' The piece failed to materialise, but Elgar certainly filled 'Caractacus' with Acland's other ideas in the most vivid way; after all the British Camp and its earthworks were part of the range of the Hills looming over the golf course.

*

Townshend's next chapter takes up the question of putting, again recommending a home-grown method of self-improvement, the setting up of a nine-hole course in the garden. (The large garden of his house on the Banbury Road in north Oxford evidently did service for a variety of sporting activities). Characteristically he goes on to suggest that the holes be played in random order, thus making each putt a fresh challenge.

As far back as 1888 the Worcestershire Golf Club had received proposals for the foundation of a Ladies' Club, and after a little initial reluctance on the part of an all-male establishment, the new development, a completely separate Club with its own clubhouse and playing area, was set up in 1891. The golfing ladies were brave. The Victorian authoress of 'The Gentlewomens' Book of Sports' wrote that 'a damsel with even one modest putter in her hand was labelled a fast and almost disreputable person.' As with cycling, appropriate dress became an issue and the game played its part in the emancipation of women. Townshend seems anxious to include them in his golfing pedagogy right from the first paragraph of 'Inspired Golf.'

He concludes his chapter on putting by advising a gentleman to practise this part of the game with a lady player, taking her as a partner to challenge a bogey score for each hole if he is anxious about either the lack of chivalry involved in beating her, or the humiliation of being beaten by her. As the author well knew, there is nothing like a respectable classical reference to obliterate such petty concerns. Amaryllis, the shepherdess figure of Theocritus, Virgil and Ovid, gives her name to the chapter.

CHAPTER SEVEN: AMARYLLIS IN THE GARDEN

I cannot claim to be the first to apply the word inspiration to golf, for putting by itself is an inspiration, as some one before me has well remarked; and I fancy some of us know the happy feeling of being truly inspired on those glorious days when all our putts seem to go right of themselves. Alas! those occasions are painfully rare compared to the less happy but too oft-recurring days when our putts either mostly go wrong or, if right, seem to get there by a pure fluke. Now, the question is, does inspiration of the special brand I advocate help towards this truly inspired putting or the reverse?

Personally I cannot declare positively that it does help; but this much I will say: my inspiration, by which I mean striking the ball with the lungs filled and the breath held, does undoubtedly tend to keep the head still, and in putting the importance of keeping the head still is the one point on which all the golfing authorities that I have ever heard of are agreed. Except on that single point the teachers of golf disagree more or less in their doctrines about putting, and where great doctors disagree I most assuredly am not going to be so presumptuous as to trot out any private prescription of my own. Or, if I did, it would have to be a mere vague aphorism, a generalisation such as certain quacks love to ladle out, something couched in this sort of style: "There is no bad putting, there is only wrong thinking, wrong belief."

This does sound like quackery, but all the same the dictum really has a core of value hidden in it, just as some appalling quacks have unquestionably got hold of very real truths. Only believe in your heart that you can putt; only force yourself to have faith; your long putts will veritably go as dead as Colonel Bogey's, your short putts will go in. Quackery or not, that this is true I from my heart believe; nevertheless it does not quite solve the problem, because even as you look steadily at the ball and draw back the putter to strike, how are you to tell whether you do actually believe or whether your forced faith is no more than a make-believe? For there are two sides to your brain, and while one says, "I believe," the other may sneer aside, "Self-deceiver, you don't!"

So there you are. Faith is the solution, but who can show us the recipe for getting faith? Every one of us knows that if only he has the confidence he can putt with any thing at all in the shape of a putter, be it of iron, aluminium, or wood, be it made with an upright lie or a flat lie, with a long shaft or with a short one; ay, he can putt with a walking-stick or an umbrella handle if it comes to that; nothing matters if only you can and do believe that you can. Potes quia posse videris.

But though I dare offer you no recipe for getting faith, O weak brother, I may say a word or two as to practice. One way of salvation for players such as you and I are is to practise hard at our putting, and the plan that I recommend to you is to keep a private spook, a Bogey Colonel of your own, and play against him, provided that, as with all other practising, you don't go on too long and get stale. Remember that great aphorism of Voltaire's about education: "Every method is good except the one that bores you." Don't let your putting practice be a bore, then. Make a course in your garden and see in what score you can do the round of six or nine or twelve holes, taking two strokes a hole as your bogey.

Merely striking a lot of balls at a hole, hit or miss, is no use. You must play a whole round to score, and play against a recognized ideal. Then, when you have begun by holing, say, three holes in or under bogey, it becomes a real effort to keep it up and go on to hole the remaining three, or six, or nine, or whatever number of holes you may have agreed on with yourself as the complete round, without letting The Terrible Colonel beat you. Such practice is far more useful than knocking balls casually into holes, it is also more amusing, and of course it is best of all when you can get a friendly opponent to oblige by taking you on.

Supposing that you find a partner for your garden golf you may make the game infinitely more varied and interesting by the following scheme. Let us say that you have laid out a course of nine holes on a lawn the size of a tennis ground. Give each of the nine holes its own name, Kop, Pisgah, Centre, and so on; you must then write each name on a small square of cardboard, and put the lot of them in your pocket. Stand at one end of the lawn and at haphazard draw a name from your pocket. You and your partner then have to tee up where you are standing and play to the hole you have drawn. As soon as you have holed out there, draw another name, tee up beside the hole just played, and play to the one you have now drawn. When the holes have all been drawn and played you will have done a nine-hole round which had this excitement about it, that when you started it you had and could have no knowledge as to the order in which the holes were going to come or as to their length. Rounds thus played would practically never come two alike, and consequently you must be studying fresh putts every time, seeing that the length of each hole will depend on how far it lies from the one drawn immediately before. If instead of doing this you always play the same nine-hole course you get too cunning, experience teaching you the strength of every putt over well; but this simple device of drawing holes by lot instead of playing them in a fixed order affords an infinite variety, and makes it much more like actual play on the links.

As physical strength counts for just nothing on the putting green a lady partner (if you are lucky enough to find one) may give you just as good a match as a man. But if you find that when playing with a lady you are conscious of a natural repugnance to beating her (or being beaten by her!) try taking her as a partner and making Colonel Bogey play your best ball. If that arrangement makes the battle too easy for the pair of you combined, you may even concede him a point, possibly even two points, in order to produce a desperate fight, but the Terrible Colonel is apt to be a stiff proposition anyhow. Take him on, then, and back up your partner bravely in her struggle. Never mind if the Colonel does beat you; after all there is no harm done. Even if you have not sported with Amaryllis in the shade, you have played golf with her in the garden, and like a certain noble Roman you may write on your tablets, "Diem hunc non perdidi." "I have not lost to-day." And did you not enjoy yourself the better for her company? I used once to know out in the Far West a certain truly sporting tribe of Red Indians (not yet, I hope, quite extinct), who had a fine saying, "No happiness without a woman!" But I fear there are golfers who would hardly subscribe to that sentiment on the links.

Interlude 1899: 'More Power to Your Elbow'

Soon after the first performance of 'Caractacus' in the October of 1898, Elgar, had begun to sketch the music of his first masterpiece, the Variations for Orchestra known as 'Enigma.' Each variation was to be a musical portrait of a friend, headed by their initials or a nickname, and the work includes three of Elgar's golfing partners, Basil Nevinson - 'BGN' - Richard Arnold, - 'RPA' - and of course Richard Baxter Townshend – 'RBT.' His music was based on an incident at a Hasfield Court house-party, when Townshend had been persuaded 'faute de mieux' and rather against his will, to attempt the rôle of an old man in some amateur theatricals. The audience was struck by his efforts to adopt a low voice for the part. RBT's normal voice was almost falsetto, sounding as if it had never broken, and he kept lapsing into it to the amusement of all. Elgar's reaction was to call him 'the delight-maker,' and to those 'in the know' his musical version of the occasion was immediately funny. Minnie's step-daughter Dora remembered laughing the first time she heard Elgar play the music on the piano, although she could not say why, and William Baker was so struck by the likeness of the music to his brother-in-law that all he could say at the first performance was 'Well, I'm damned!'

Some years later RBT asked Dora to explain how his music was like him and why Baker had reacted as he did. It was rather an embarrassing position to be in, but she did the best she could. 'That's no end interesting,' replied the completely unmusical Townshend, 'but I wish I could see it just as you do!' People have in fact tried to 'see it' in all kinds of different ways, finding suggestions of riding over the wide-open prairies in the music, as well as of tricycles and ringing bells. Dora thought that the opening mimicked his way of starting a conversation for he 'had a curious didactic manner of speaking.' She also heard another of RBT's mannerisms in the music, his habit of saying assertively after one of his cowboy tales had found an unappreciative listener, 'Damn and blast it, man! Can't you understand what I'm telling you?' Other people have described the piece as being a slightly weird kind of dance, a sort of waltz or mazurka. But nobody has heard the smack of club against golfball in it – yet.

Elgar worked at the Enigma music into the early part of 1899. On 11th January Richard Arnold wrote to Alice enclosing an edition of his father's poems, and asked her to pass a message to her busy husband. 'Please give him my best love, & ask him if he saw the notice in the Telegraph yesterday about the new and fashionable disease, called golficitis – no respectable composer should be without it.' And the 'respectable composer' was able to fit three rounds in while orchestrating the Variations between the fifth and nineteenth of February. The golf would have been the perfect antidote to long hours spent sitting over the thousands of notes he had to write legibly for the publisher.

For some time now Alice had been eager to move, and in March the Elgars began life at a large handsome house he dubbed 'Craeg Lea' at Malvern Wells, just at the top of the Common. The Golf Club was now much nearer, just a short walk away, and at the end of the month RBT came to stay for a few days by way of celebration. On 29th he and Elgar again spent all day on the course.

Taking his life in his hands, Elgar had sent the Variations to the then greatest living conductor, the German Hans Richter. He agreed to give their first performance in London, a real boost for a provincial musician who was still having to teach. The work established

Elgar's reputation and is still regarded by some critics as the greatest orchestral work yet written by an Englishman. Unmusical as he may have been, RBT understood the importance of the successful reception gained by the Variations for the future of Elgar's career, and he wrote a warm, encouraging letter of congratulation to the composer, full of characteristic dynamism and informality not to mention his favourite v-words.

'My dear Elgar, I must just put in a line to say in my native Irish 'more power to your elbow.' I am glad that it has gone so well and that people have tumbled to it. Do go ahead my dear fellow with vim vinegar and vitriol and just make things hum. This is not my native Irish but my second-nature American and it means just the same. If I was to say 'Macte non virtute puer sic itur ad astra' it would express the sentiment only in a more classical style. I think you must be feeling rather good just now, and just want to say hurrah. Ever yours, R. B. Townshend.'

*

Back to experimental psychology. 'Inspired Golf' now continues with a chapter suggesting that there is much to be learnt by the thoughtful player who reverses things completely and plays left–handed. Analysis should then enable what Townshend calls the 'observing mind' to understand the various details better. But significantly he goes on to add a rider, not for the first time, not to force the issue, and to drop the idea if it becomes a chore.

Lost ball – the invariable Enigma

CHAPTER EIGHT: AMBIDEXTERITY

And now let us leave our putting with Amaryllis in the garden for a while and switch off the train of our ideas to quite another line. I have said that the real difficulty you want to overcome in golf is mental, seeing that what is required of you is the concentrated effort of mind needful alike in order to recognise your faults and to amend them; also we saw that for this purpose an outside view of your swing can be a great help, and that the weak brother would be well advised to get the sun at his back so that he may be enabled to detect his faults as they are faithfully repeated by his shadow. This shadow image of yourself certainly lends an effectual aid to visualising the various positions successively occupied by the head, body, hands, and feet, in the process of delivering the blow, but at the same time it can hardly help you much towards the mental analysis of the mysterious reasons why your arms and legs should insist on getting themselves into the various false positions they incline to fall into. There is a method, however, which some of us have found helpful towards this analysis, namely, to reverse every one of the bodily positions by striking the ball left-handed. The inversion enables the observing mind to follow the details of the action much closer.

To make trial of what is in fact a very simple experiment borrow a club from an amiable left-handed friend and tee up, that is if you can harden your heart and persuade yourself to take a full left-handed shot at a solid ball, or you may simply try a swing or two at a daisy with the back of one of your own right-handed clubs Don't worry over it, but slash away cheerfully, remembering that if the result of the experiment pleases you it will be a simple thing to buy a few old left-handed clubs cheap either from a professional or through the exchange columns of a newspaper, and so go into the thing properly equipped on your own.

Assuming that a confiding friend has lent you one of his clubs, tee up with care and address your ball left-handed. Here, by the way, let me insert a caution. If you are using captive balls be sure the string that restrains their flight lies pointing well forward as you address the ball. If it does not, the clubhead is liable to entangle itself in the string and then the ball becomes like a certain Hebrew prophet according to Voltaire, *capable de tout.* It may come right round and hit you very hard on the head, or fly off behind you and break somebody else's head, or it may only break a window, but it is pretty sure to do some mischief or other. You have to look out for this when you are striking in the ordinary way, but it is particularly likely to happen when you start on so awkward a thing as striking off left-handed. Also I would say, and this is most important if the club is a borrowed one, don't tee the captive ball so that the club can possibly strike against the nail or staple to which the string is fastened. If you do you will find that a strongly marked impression has been made on the face of that club, and the owner won't love you much for that!

So tee up, as I said, "with care," which is the way the caddies at "Westward Ho!" were of old taught to do, and keep your weather eye open to see how you are going to shape as a left-hander. If you happen to be naturally ambidexterous, even the first blow will quite possibly be all right, only unfortunately nature's plan is to make very few of us after that highly-desirable double-action run-both-ways pattern. The famous founder of the Boy Scouts is said to have such perfect ambidexterity that he can write two letters to two different people at once, one with his right hand and one with his left; but then he belongs to the class of the "rara avis" described by the old Roman writer as "most like to a black swan."

No; more probably your first attempt at a full drive left-handed will end (like the marriage service) in amazement; you will hear the club whistle through the empty air and behold the ball, still teed up in situ, looking you meekly in the face. At this sight old memories will revive, carrying you back to your first week of golf, when you not rarely missed the globe altogether without having the ghost of an idea why. Be consoled, then, for missing some of your early left-handed shots and persevere; you will find yourself hitting them presently, and probably surprise yourself by finding how correct the form of your left-handed finish can be, even though the ball may travel but a little distance. Why the ball should not fly farther when the swing seems correct is hard to say; it may be due to the weakness of the left arm, or to the feebler grip of the left fingers; but you will be doing uncommonly well if one shot in twenty goes anywhere near as far as your ordinary right-handed blow. The distance that you get, however, is not of real importance; the point is to utilise the strangeness of the reversed position of the body so that the mind can analyse the details of its movements and educate itself to carry on the same analysis still more effectually when you return to right-handed striking. Concentrate on this, and experiment not only with a driver but with the other clubs.

Let me repeat, don't worry yourself in the slightest over this left-handed golf: if it amuses and interests you, well and good; go on with it as long as it continues to do so. If you keep it up for a couple of weeks there is no reason why you should not make a match with another weak brother (or sister), one it may well be even weaker than yourself, and go out and play a whole round with nothing but left-handed clubs in your bag. I will venture a guess that you will be mightily pleased if at the end of the eighteen holes your score is not something a bit worse than sevens.

But the moment left-handed golf bores you, drop it like hot potato. I am not recommending the thing to you as a penance, however much you may deserve to do penance for your golfing sins, and however able and willing you may be to scourge yourself down the back with a left-handed club in the most approved Penitente fashion. The Penitente performer, whose bleeding back surprised me so that day in New Mexico I have told of, was almost as ambidexterous as the founder of the Boy Scouts himself, so much so that he criss-crossed his lacerated skin with alternate right and left-handed strokes, laid on most impartially. But then he wasn't doing it to amuse himself; that I can swear to; whereas you, O weak brother, I hope, are getting some pleasure out of the attempt to find a cure for your sins; if you can't enjoy yourself when you are playing a game, it is about time for your to get off the planet.

So long as it amuses you, then, practise the method of inversion, and remember that the ability to play a left-handed shot may sometimes be really useful. When I was teaching rifle-shooting (another of my hobbies) I always urged my young friends to shoot from the left shoulder as well as from the right. They may find it convenient some day to aim thus round the left-hand angle of a wall without having to expose the whole body, while on horse-back it is the only way to fire off your weapon squarely to the right except by the awkward plan of holding the rifle as a pistol. So with a golf ball: some day you may discover yours in a bunker where you can't get at it right-handed at all, but where a left-handed club, if you have one and can use it, may land you safely on the fair-way. After blundering into a bunker, a triumphant extrication like that puts you in heart again. You need not despise ambidexterity.

Interlude 1900: Two Wonderful Scores

At the beginning of January Elgar agreed to compose a work to be performed in October at the prestigious Birmingham Festival. It was to be a setting of Cardinal Newman's 'The Dream of Gerontius,' and although the composer had already been considering the piece for a long time, the burden of work, against tight rehearsal deadlines, and with much complicated proof-correcting, was enormous. He had to work almost non-stop until August to make sure the music was ready on time.

But there was to be no lessening of golf that year, quite the opposite in fact. Alice's diary records no less than seventy-one visits to the Club, which makes 1900 Elgar's second most active golfing year, outdone only by 1894 with eighty-seven. And it got off to a rather auspicious start, as Alice related on 6th February, when Elgar played a three-ball match: 'E. played with Carr &Paterson did 16th hole in 2 Mirabile dictu.' It is his best-known score for a hole, and it found its way into the Club records. The sixteenth, by no means and easy one to tackle, was a 230-yard hole running alongside the Great Western Railway line. The 'Gerontius' score prospered too, and the composer was able to send off some of the first part of the music to the publishers on 2nd March, and the remainder on 20th. Under all the pressure, golfing and composing were going together, in fact, for Alice's diary tells us that Elgar played golf on the 3rd, 5th, 6th, 7th, 8th, 10th, 12th, 15th, 17th and 20th March, as well as on another three occasions before the end of the month.

One occasion on which he did not play golf that month was during a visit on the 29th from his friend and sparring partner the composer Granville Bantock, whose new and exotic Symphonic Poem 'Jaga-Naut' had just been given its first performance. He and Elgar, two up-and–coming English composers with a shared if somewhat schoolboy sense of humour, frequently discussed matters which they had in common, such as the merits or demerits of music critics, or their favourite pipe tobaccos, but golf was not one of them. Bantock wrote in advance to arrange his visit.

. . . I shall expect to come over to worry you on Thursday morning by the 9.37 GWR arriving Malvern at 11.7 – just in time to sniff at the "Arcadian Mixture." But I cannot stand cut-plug, especially when anyone else smokes it, unless I have my own pipe full of it, and worse luck – I find I've completely run out of the divine juice, so shall have to content myself with common plain democratic hand-cut-virginia-unscented. To avoid your mal-odorous pipes & particularly the "Evening Glow" mixture, which sounds suspiciously as if saltpetre formed an important ingredient, I propose returning straight home by the 5.25 arriving Lpool at 9.20, unless I should have to go to London. But I am afraid I shall be keeping you from the studs, links – which are they? – and only wild horses would drag me to commit such an act of wanton folly as to be guilty of watching & abetting you in ye mischievous game of "hit-ball-and-walk-after." The farthing rags are shrieking at my brutality in daring to picture Jaga-Naut, & one Solon describes my poor rubbish as glorified pantomime music!!!?=+"÷X£$&-;! Let not the enigma of these symbols be breathed aloud.

So Elgar had to leave the clubs at home that day and be content with taking Bantock for an afternoon walk on the Hills.

Exactly how much of 'Gerontius' was composed on the golf course with its magnificent panorama of the Malverns we shall never know, but Elgar often jotted down musical ideas in the open air and he once sent a couple of bars of music to a friend, saying they were 'made probably on the golf links.' It was music from 'Gerontius,' what the composer described as 'a certain appalling chord' which introduces the Angel of the Agony in Part Two as he sings: 'Jesu! By that shudd'ring dread which fell on Thee . . .'

Or perhaps another mental mechanism was at work, for the composer told his first biographer that he thought golf was a grand game because you couldn't think of any thing else while playing. That could be a help in any kind of creative undertaking because the subconscious mind continues the work all the time, and you can find on returning to the task in hand that problems have solved themselves and you forge ahead.

Elgar was poorly for most of April, plagued with a cough and cold and under the doctor's care. The Elgars' ten year-old daughter, Carice also became unwell. He was missing his golf and twice managed to get down to the Club, but only to 'look on.' RBT came to the rescue with a cheery letter from Hasfield Court; he had been tickled by Elgar's having confided his intention to cipher the names of people he disliked into the notes of the Demons' Chorus in 'Gerontius.'

'My dear Elgar, I want to send you a picture of me dropping large tears at hearing of the woeful plagues that beset your house. I fancy that's quite Aeschylean style at the end of the paragraph. But you make me laugh so consumedly with your jests and your hopes of being able to put your enemies into H-ll with new Op. spoil it quite. But you are mending (I hope) all of you and if so be I will try to drop in on you on April 25th (if you really be mended) when the brutal 10/- a day will (I hope) no longer be extracted from the unhappy Uitlander golfer in Malvern. My address till that date is expected to be at Hawse End, Keswick. More power to your elbow. Give it to those enemies. So glad I ain't one! Ever your affectionate, R.B. Townshend.'

History does not record if the 'brutal' ten shillings a day fee for visitors was in fact extracted, but RBT managed a visit on 26th April, encouraging Elgar to play his first golf for some weeks, and returning to Craeg Lea afterwards for tea. Later that day Alice found her husband 'writing vehemently,' and golf and 'Gerontius' continued together until the work was finished at the beginning of June. On May 14th Alice's diary tells us 'E. busy writing. E. to Links;' on 22nd May 'E. hard writing. To links played with Mr. Arnold;' on 29th May 'E. to Links – very hard at last Chorus,' and the next day 'E. to Links. Nearly finished great chorus.' And Elgar played on 1st, 2nd, 4th and 5th of June, before finishing the final instalment on 6th.

After a few days' break in London, Elgar now began to tackle the orchestration, with regular golf as before. By now he had been fully accepted by his non-musical golfing friends. On 28th June, for example, Alice noted 'Mr Paterson dined here.' It was part of a pattern, and by this time such names as Jones, Carr and Hookham, with their ladies, had all appeared in the diary as being invited to tea or dinner, and had reciprocated the invitations. Everybody was happy to know Elgar now.

That summer the Elgars removed to a 'working retreat' cottage at Storridge, north of Malvern, too far from the golf course for regular play, and the composer did not resume the game until the autumn. He worked hard at orchestrating the new music and found another mode of exercise which was even more ready to hand than golf – cycling. The 'Gerontius' score was finished early in August, and the music was distributed as quickly as possible to the performers. But its unfamiliar, difficult style caused problems, and with many other new works to be performed at the Festival, 'Gerontius' was not given adequate rehearsal. As a result the performance was very poor, often noticeably out of tune and lacking in proper ensemble. The shambolic first performance of a masterpiece has gained the reputation of being one of the most notorious disasters of English music. Even though many listeners and critics were immediately able to perceive the greatness of the music despite everything, Elgar was heartbroken, and furious. 'I have worked hard for forty years &, at the last, Providence denies me a decent hearing of my work,' he thundered in a letter to a friend. 'I always said God was against art & I still believe it. Anything obscene or trivial is blessed in this world & has a reward – I ask for no reward – only to live & to hear my work.' The iron had entered his soul.

But despite the crushing disappointment, some things could always be relied upon. He continued his letter, 'I am very well & what is called 'fit' & had my golf in good style yesterday . . .' And there was some welcome recognition in the post a few days later, when a letter arrived from Cambridge University offering Elgar an honorary degree. One who wrote to congratulate was Dyke Acland, knowing his early faith vindicated.

My dear Elgar, I am so glad that you have received an 'outward & visible sign' of recognition of your standing in the musical world, though I do not know which is more honoured,, the givers or the receiver, but at any rate I trust that it is only the first of many such recognitions. Yours very truly, H. D. Acland.

*

As he himself freely admits, there is not much philosophy in Townshend's next chapter on the philosophy of golf, except of the more homespun kind. He advises patience and moderation of language in that most notorious of golf's pitfalls, the bunker, quoting the behaviour of John Ball, eight times British Amateur Champion, and recommends the use of the punch-ball as the least boring way of keeping fit for the game. Finally there is a vignette of a Townshend nephew under instruction, and his own statement of golfing philosophy. ('Out of the mouths of babes and sucklings . . .')

I was lucky to make contact some years ago with another relative, a great-nephew, Bernard Keeling, who was a pupil at the Dragon School, Oxford, near to Townshend's house, in the early nineteen-twenties. He was several times invited to meals, and recalled, 'He was a very genial and amusing old boy. I remember that he taught me to lasso in his garden. This accommodated a wooden horse – basically a barrel. There is a photo of me astride it; presumably one practised lassoing from it.'

Putting on a nine-hole course, lassoing from a barrel, rifle practice from wooden horses - so much seemed to be going on in Townshend's garden that one might be forgiven for wondering if any of the more usual horticultural practices ever got a look-in. One tiny piece of evidence that they did is contained in Townshend's will, drawn up in 1921, two years before he died. One of the witnesses was a certain Arthur Beacham, of Green Street, Cowley, 'Gardener.' He must have been a very tolerant man, with a philosophy of golf all his own, used to dealing with scarred turf, collecting spent cartridges and providing lengths of rubber hose to be cut up for tees.

Torrents in Summer

CHAPTER NINE: THE PHILOSOPHY OF GOLF

"There are no snakes in Ireland," wrote the old monk when he began his celebrated chapter, and in like manner I would begin this by saying, "There is no philosophy of golf." At any rate, if there be such a thing, the best definition of it would be that given by an unhappy Oxford undergraduate in his viva voce in Divinity when the examiners invited him to define Original Sin. "It is," he answered, "a fond thing, vainly invented, grounded on no certain warranty of Scripture . . ." He never finished his sentence, being promptly ploughed for irreverence by the indignant dons.

Yet I hold that a golfer is bound to be a philosopher of sorts. There was another celebrated question once put at Oxford: "Could a good man be happy on the rack? " To which the reply was "Possibly, if he was a very good man, and if it was a very bad rack."

The question (and the answer?) may be altered on the links into "Can a good golfer be happy in a bunker? " If he can (and if the bunker be a very bad bunker!) then beyond a doubt he is a good philosopher. What a true philosopher would say under such trying circumstances I hardly know, but there is a story of Mr. John Ball, junior, who, playing in a championship, bunkered himself, failed to get out in one; tried again, and failed in two; and was heard to murmur as he addressed his ball for the third time, "What a silly old ass it is!"

If that was not true philosophy I never heard of anything half so well deserving of the name. Most assuredly if there be one thing certain about golf it is that you will sometimes find it very hard to keep your temper, more particularly in a bunker; but you had better keep it, if you can, as did he. We all know this well enough; the difficulty lies in the doing of it; while as for ladling out screeds of advice on the subject to you, O weak brother, well, who am I to preach? Indeed I have said some things in bunkers myself. Nay, even great professors, not of golf but of philosophy, can say things in a bunker that it would hardly do to print here.

There is a legend in a certain golf club I know of concerning the cause of the abrupt termination of the right of the club to use a piece of land which was private property. The property owner, a citizen of credit and renown, had a worthy dame, who happened one day to be innocently taking the air in the immediate vicinity of the golf course, when her ears were scandalised by words of wrath issuing from a neighbouring bunker. In the bunker a struggle was going on between a distinguished elderly philosopher and a golf ball, and the winged words that issued from it were such that the lady fled in horror, with the result that the lease of the course was never renewed. I give this legend with the caution that legends are not always founded on fact. It is only fair to add that there is a totally different version of the story current (among the senior club members) in which the whole blame is transferred from professorial shoulders to those of certain juniors; this, as Herodotus says, I know but may not relate.

It is sound philosophy for the golfer to keep himself in health by proper exercise, but he need not go into such hard training as our boxers and runners. Their violent exertions require the heart and lungs to be fit to work at concert pitch, but the links make no great demand on those organs. All the golfer needs is to have his eye clear, his muscles elastic, and his nerves right. It can do him no harm, however, and may do him good, if he does a few physical exercises at home; but how is one to select among the many much advertised systems that are in vogue? Dumbells and Indian clubs, Swedish or Danish stretching and bending movements, gymnastics and elastic cord pullers, they are all good, that is if you can be at the bother of keeping them going. For they are contrary to Voltaire's maxim; they are dull, all of them, dull as ditch-water, beyond a doubt. On this account, if I may venture personally to recommend anything, I would like to put in a word for the punching ball. To begin with, I know no better form of physical exercise; and it has a special interest of its own in this way, that the ball hits back at you, which dumbells and Indian clubs and the like never do; if you don't dodge it as it rebounds from the ceiling you may get a clip on the nose that will surely waken you up. Moreover there is one way of using it that has some points very much in common with the full shot at golf; the way is this: strike the ball as hard as ever you can and see how many times you can make it rebound. The actual number of rebounds will depend upon the weight and elasticity of the ball and the length of the string by which it is suspended as well as on the force of your punch, but you will soon find out what number of rebounds constitutes your private bogey, and ambition will make you want to beat it every time you punch. I compare this way of using the punching ball to the full shot at golf because in both you look calmly at the passive ball waiting there for you to strike; calmly you waggle or measure your distance; and then finally you let go at it with every ounce of strength you have got; you follow through; and afterwards you stand by to watch the effect. Say your particular bogey with the punching ball is ten rebounds; any sort of punch will give you eight, which is no better than a foozle; to get nine you must hit the ball square in the middle and get your body well behind the blow; but when it bumps the ceiling for the tenth time you know you have got in a screamer. As you have to wait for half a minute to count the rebounds the delay involved just gives you time to collect your strength for the next shot; you stop the ball and bring it to rest, and then go at it again. Only when you get your whole force into it and hit the ball perfectly true have you a chance of doing your bogey score of ten. And every time as you gather yourself to strike the hope springs up in you that this time you may surpass yourself, and do an eleven. For these reasons I say that ball-punching has something in common with the golfing drive and may therefore prove worth your attention.

As the parson said in his sermon, one word more and I have done. Do not let your practice be continued long enough to be a bore, but do let it be done in close connection with your reading on the subject, or in other words, combine practice and theory. So did the immortal Mr. Squeers expound his method, "c-l-e-a-n, clean, verb active, to make bright, to scour. W-i-n, win, d-e-r, der, winder, a casement. When the boy knows this out of a book, he goes and does it."

How did such a horrible beast as Squeers get hold of the true philosophy of education? For such precisely is what that admirable principle of his amounts to.

However, it is time to call a truce to philosophy. I have headed this chapter, "the philosophy of golf," thought looking back now I can't see that there is much philosophy in it, but that perhaps is no great loss, for we are apt to talk (or write) too much about the hows and whys of most things; in time-honoured phrase it is better to cut the gab and come to the 'osses. I remember once taking out a nephew of mine, a hopeful youth, to give him a little instruction in the art of golf, and naturally proceeded to lay down the whole law about body-swing, and finger-grip, and keeping the head still, and following through, much as I have done above. The youth listened awhile with attention, and then cut me short with, "Why, uncle, all you've got to do is to look at the ball, and hit it!"

I think he hit it that time.

Interlude 1901-1903: 'Smite the Knave over the Costard . . .'

Fame continued to make many inroads on Elgar's time, and his remaining years in Malvern saw a gradual reduction of golf. He began to travel more frequently to accept conducting engagements, gained a new circle of London-based friends, and enjoyed a winter in Italy on the proceeds of his new Oratorio, 'The Apostles.' Other well-known works were composed during this period, including the 'Cockaigne' Overture and the first two 'Pomp & Circumstance' Marches, and cycling continued to be a primary source of exercise and musical inspiration. Nevertheless golf, as Elgar said, was always ready to hand when the mood beckoned. On 4th February, 1901, he once again braved a snowstorm to go down to the course, and two days later, despite it being 'very cold,' music and golf went together again when he spent one part of the day playing and the rest working on 'Cockaigne.' A publisher - a German one - was finally found for the 1894 Worcester Cathedral piece, 'Sursum Corda' and Elgar dedicated the work to Dyke Acland, acknowledging his friend's help and support in both golfing and musical matters. The banker was shortly to leave Malvern and spend a considerable amount of time travelling abroad, and in the letter of thanks he made sure to write to the composer when his copy of the music arrived, he showed that their good friendship owed something to 'Amaryllis.' 'My dear Elgar,' he wrote, 'When I came home I found the 'parcel' and I am proud to think that my name should appear on your composition which is so closely associated in my memory with Worcester Cathedral. The friendship that has existed between my wife and yours from the earliest days of our life in Malvern – now as you may have heard fast drawing to an end – has been so happily cemented by that between the husbands . . . I shall look all the more eagerly for notices of your work, and the still wider recognition of your musicianship.'

And golf brought out something of the spirit of the first 'Pomp & Circumstance' March in Elgar when he played the piece to Dora one day in May. That evening he came down for dinner wearing a bright red golf blazer with brass buttons instead of his usual formal evening wear. Some years before, there had been some discussion by the Club Committee about the adoption of exactly such a uniform blazer by members, but the matter seems to have remained undecided. In the wider golfing world, opinion was divided between those who regarded the red coat as a sign of proficiency, and those who saw it as a warning of exactly the opposite, and on a course such as that of the Worcestershire Club, on common land to which everyone had access, safety would be an important consideration. Quite what factor might have operated in Elgar's case, we will not enquire too deeply. That month also brought a superb performance of the 'Enigma' Variations in London, attended by both Elgars and various musical friends, who repaired afterwards to the Langham Hotel for tea. Dyke Acland was present, and he once again wrote of his pride in the recognition being awarded to his fellow-golfer. The effect that Elgar's music could have on an audience was often remarkable; Acland was struck by the way they all rose at the end of the work and shouted for the composer, and he remarked on the unity of the strings and the way that fifteen cellos 'sang out that air' in Basil Nevinson's Variation.

There was always RBT to be relied on for purely golfing encouragement, of course, and he was still keen to do what he could to improve Elgar's play. 'I would I had you on our links with those clubs and doing the true St. Andrew's swing,' he wrote in December. 'That's my form. I feel older, alas! but I try to "follow through" still. I think we go to Hasfield for Xmas and if so I must make a desperate effort to get around to Craeg Lea be the wild winds what they may.' But the Elgars were in Germany that Christmas for a performance of 'Gerontius.'

Two pro forma letters from the Club to Elgar survive from February, 1902, both headed 'Notice,' in formal capital letters. The first one requested members 'to pick out, and remove, from the heap of old clothes up stairs, such things as they wish to keep. After 1ˢᵗ June the residue will be given to some charity.' The second, no less peremptory, ran 'Members who are entitled to a locker are requested to see that their names are on their locker before the 10ᵗʰ March, as on that day all doubtful lockers will be emptied.' To which Elgar added his own somewhat enigmatic comment in green ink, 'some lockers are more 'doubtful' when named – see the Committee Room.' Could it be that some of the worthy and distinguished members of the Committee did not entirely meet with the composer's approval? But his golfing partners continued to be the established ones, Carr, Jones, Patterson and 'old Hookham,' as Alice called him, and there were frequent 'fearsomes' that year. 1902, in fact, saw Elgar tasting the agonies and ecstasies of the game. For once Alice gives us one of his scores for a round, when she tells us that on 10ᵗʰ February he achieved an 86. It must have been a good score for it to be considered worthy of mention. Perhaps it was his best ever; 'great joy,' she added. But three days later, after he had been to London to confer about the 'Coronation Ode' he was to write for Edward VII, it was a case of 'E. to Links did not play so well.' What depths of misery lay behind that short sentence can only be guessed at.

Elgar's friendship with the Bakers and Townshends contained much scope for humour. 'Oh, me, it does me good to hear you make a joke again, not that we are too blessed serious here in Oxford,' RBT wrote to his golfing protégé. One of Elgar's jokes was a long-running historical charade of Royalists against Roundheads, played during Hasfield house-parties. William Baker's sons were Princes and Elgar was Nanty Ewart, the character in Scott's novel 'Redgauntlet,' and a Royalist sympathiser: Hasfield itself became a Fort. Both Townshends were strongly suspected of Roundhead sympathies, and Elgar thought it best to issue a warning about them in his best 'olde Englishe' style. It was perhaps typical of the literary banter that the golfers shared together.

' . . . it is sd. yt. two rebellious persones (wh. by leading outwardlie seeming quiet and respectable lives have imposed upon and hoodewink'd ye Burgesses of Oxforde) are plottinge to descende thys daye on the neighbourhd of ye Forte for purposes deadlie agt. it and, belike, agt. yr. owne persone if not ye Kings. Ye Twain travel in ye publicke wains to disarm suspicion and can easily be waylaid and quieted. Altho' one Nanty Ewart, known to yr. H'ness as a true man tho' something of a Roysterer, hathe sworne to smite the knave over the costard and to slit his weasand, and again (after his thirde can) to burie a yard of steel in his Waine. But more certaine steps shd be taken: the Fellowe is dangerous and hathe skill in the uses of ye musketoon and petronel . . .'

68

And ye golfe clubbe, Elgar might have added; a vow to 'smite the knave over the costard' might be a good enough motto for any golfer preparing to address the ball. The composer was able to smite only on some twelve occasions during 1903, and was now enough of a celebrity to be the subject of a two-page illustrated interview published in 'The Sketch' in October. The photographs included various indoor shots of the composer looking at his books, admiring the view and sitting at his writing-desk. But golf was such a part of his life, and the course so near, that he went out with Carice to be photographed while attempting some putting. Dressed in his best, Elgar looked every inch a typical, prosperous golfing countryman, plus fours now instead of gaiters. He had come a long way from the aspiring new member of ten years before, and was even the subject of a sally in 'Punch.' 'The other day,' wrote that illustrious gentleman, 'Mr Elgar gave a wonderful exhibition of his power as a driver. Slicing his tee shot at the short hole over the railway, Mr Elgar managed to land his ball in a passing motor-car, which was not stopped until it had gone half a mile . . .'

*

Townshend concludes with a chapter of delightful, kindly anecdotes, 'period pieces' all, of the Oxford University Golf Club, many of which illustrate his opening statement about 'the everlasting comedy of youth and age.' Townshend had become a member of the OUGC in 1895 with a handicap of 10. Three years previously the OUGC had played a match with the Worcestershire Club at Malvern, losing by twenty holes, somewhat to the chagrin of the University men. Their Secretary's somewhat pointed account of the venture in the minute-book emphasized that 'some of the Oxford players were much handicapped by the continuous thunder and lightning as well as by their ignorance of the course and the Malvern Club's local rules.'

RBT became Hon. Treasurer of the OUGC in 1898, and took some responsibility for the work of a sub-committee investigating extensions to the pavilion on the Hinksey course – a 'larger shop, a bicycle shed, a caddies' office (small)' and so on. At the March 1899 AGM (the one which saw the episode of student hilarity which forms one of Townshend's anecdotes), he presented his Statement of Accounts, and then 'went through each item in detail and was able to give satisfactory answers to various questions asked by members.' Two months later he took the chair at an Extraordinary General Meeting to elect a new President, but RBT's own tenure of office was to be short-lived. At the 1900 AGM, held at Exeter College, 'The Treasurer . . . made his Financial Statement and pointed out that the Club was in a most prosperous state, and regretted very much that he felt compelled to resign.' The response to an apparently somewhat mysterious decision was generous. A vote of thanks was proposed, 'showing the various valuable services that he had performed for the Club. Seconded and carried unanimously.'

Tee'd up at the 19th

CHAPTER TEN: MERE ANECDOTAGE

"Forty years on, growing older and older,
Shorter in wind but in memory long."

Yes, in memory long! That is what you, reader, will come to be also, if permitted like me to reach the threescore years and ten of the Psalmist. It is no sort of use to grumble over growing old, but one may pick and choose amid the lengthening scroll of one's memory and dwell by preference on the most cheerful of its contents. The generations pass, but the everlasting comedy of youth and age is repeated, and to be the elderly treasurer of a golf club where your committee consist mostly of young men under twenty-one has certain compensations.

For instance, I remember about the end of the last century there was a certain reverend and very highly distinguished professor, not himself a golfer, whose schoolboy sons used to play over the course in the holidays. The club fees were then I think 5/- a week for this privilege, which of course during the long holidays comes to a tidy sum; and the professor's wife wrote to the treasurer to know if the club would not let her boys have the use of their course on somewhat easier terms.

His reply was to the effect that if the professor, even though he was not himself a golfer, cared to become a member of the club, he, the treasurer, would gladly try to get the club's consent to allow his two boys to play free; and accordingly at the next meeting, after reading out the correspondence to a roomful of undergraduates forming the committee, he observed that he had drafted a rule which he thought would meet the case and begged to submit it accordingly.

This suggestion being met with favour, he proceeded to read out his proposed new rule, which began thus:

"Rule XXI. That the privilege of using the club links be extended during the vacations to the sons of members under eighteen years of age . . . "

That first sentence was never finished, being drowned in an electric burst of laughter from his young friends; and as the elderly treasurer looked up, beaming at them through his spectacles, it dawned on him that there was something about the wording of his draft that was quite too much for the gravity of irresponsible undergraduates. They passed his new rule, however, all right, but it was passed in a somewhat hastily amended form.

The relations between father and son must always have a peculiar interest for an audience made up of young men, who, far from earning their own living, are dependent on a paternal allowance. Just then the club was parting with its professional; he was a celebrated ex-champion of the great world of golf, and the club had promoted to the vacant place a very promising golfer, a young man who had been the assistant professional; he was a local youth whose old father happened to be employed in the professional's shop as a club repairer. Now the committee had made a practice of allowing the departing ex-champion, in addition to his wages, the half-time services of a boy who was paid entirely by the club but worked in the afternoons in the shop for the benefit of the professional. The privilege had not hitherto been extended to the newly-promoted assistant, who appealed to the treasurer about it. "Very well," said the latter, "I am quite willing you should have it, but I think your best plan will be to write me a letter saying exactly what you wish us to do, and I will bring the matter before the next meeting of the committee."

The letter was duly written, and the treasurer, after telling the committee about it in his own words, said: "Of course there is a certain complication in the matter, so perhaps I had better read you in full exactly what our young professional has to say about it himself."Accordingly he read out the letter, which, after recounting the extra help in the shop which had previously been allowed to the departed ex-champion, went on to say: "You see, sir, that I am left with only my father to work under me in the shop, and as I cannot very well discharge him . . ."

That sentence likewise was drowned in inextinguishable laughter. The delicate point about the difficulty of 'firing out the pater' tickled irresistibly the committee of juveniles so that they fairly exploded. However, they assented most sympathetically to the newly-made pro's application, and he was duly allowed "half a boy's time."

Golf has so completely conquered the country now that the younger generation mostly gets hold of the elements of the game in childhood; but twenty years ago it was quite otherwise, and tall, powerful athletes, coming up from school to the 'Varsity, know almost nothing of golf. I remember once, when I was striking off to the eleventh hole on the Cowley course, which is the nearer of the two University courses at Oxford, a couple of raw undergraduates were just playing to the fourth, which is exactly parallel to the eleventh hole but is played in the opposite direction, so that a badly pulled shot at either hole will leave the ball in the fairway of the other. I was walking to my ball after the drive, when I saw one of the men who were playing to the fourth turn considerably to his own left, march to where I expected mine to lie, and whack a ball from there into a yawning bunker. When I hurried to where my ball should most certainly have been lying, no ball whatever was to be seen, and I called after him with some severity, "I'm afraid you've played my ball, sir."

Back came the indignant denial: "No, indeed, sir. I've done nothing of the sort."

Then came 'whack' at the poor thing reposing helpless in the bunker below him, and 'whack' again, and then a third blow which fetched the victim of wrath out on to the green. Meantime, not finding mine, I hurried after the culprit, stopped him as he was preparing for yet another blow, pointed to the woefully scarred ball, and said, "If you'll look at that thing I think you'll find my initials on it." He stooped and picked it up.

"Oh, so it is! I say, sir, I'm awfully sorry! I hadn't the least idea. And I've knocked it about frightfully! Look here, sir, have another . . ." and the ingenuous youth, diving into a side pocket, produced a brand-new ball which he tried hard to get me to accept. I believe he was really contrite and dismissed him with my blessing.

The Oxford atmosphere is sometimes accused of fostering rather alarming socialistic tendencies among its youth, and it is true that the doctrine of community of goods finds a certain acceptance with junior members of the University. I remember once walking up to the club-house on the old Hinksey links, the first day of term, just to see how things were. Not many of the young men had come up to the course so soon, but one of those that had done so was an undergraduate whose native heath was Hoylake, the second-best course in England, and who occasionally condescended to give me a liberal allowance of strokes and a beating.

"Would you care for a game, sir?" he asked, seeing me there without a partner.

"Very much," I replied, "but I've been away for the vacation and I haven't brought my clubs with me to-day."

"Oh," said he, "if you didn't mind playing with strange clubs I think I could fit you out"; and I watched him pop into one undergraduate locker after another, extracting a driver here, a brassy there, and a variety of irons elsewhere, till he had got together a goodly set. "perhaps these might suit you, sir," he smiled, "and then we could have a round."

We had it, and I only hope that if ever the lawful owners got those clubs back they found them not very much the worse for wear. Nor is it undergraduates alone who play a part in our eternal comedy of youth and age. Caddy boys also come on to the stage; though at Oxford we do not have many of them, as the younger men mostly prefer to carry their own clubs. I knew once a professor who went out for a game with a friend, both of them being Irish and (occasionally) given to picturesque exaggeration. They struck off; and their performances were anything but brilliant, it must be confessed, at the first couple of holes; and then as they walked to the third tee the professor gaily remarked, "I shan't be able to give you any thing of a match to-day, old chap, I was beastly drunk last night."

"You don't come that over me," retorted his friend. "Last night I was at a College Gaudy and I had a good skinful of champagne." And then it suddenly dawned on him that to-day as it chanced he had taken out a caddy, a very rare thing with him. And remembering also Horace's famous line, "Maxima debetur puero reverentia" he turned sharp round to the smug-faced urchin at his heels with, "We don't really mean it, you know."

"Oh, NO, sir," came the prompt answer of the wily infant; but the unbelieving grin with which he uttered those three words revealed the real opinion of his class as to the true moral character of senior members of the University Golf Club.

Elgar scores a birdie

Finale: 'The Most Appalling Golf Shot I Have Ever Seen.'

If 1904 proved Elgar's grandest year yet, it was one which marked the beginning of the end as far as his game was concerned. He did not visit the Club until April, when he played just twice. The delay had been caused by a winter holiday in Italy extending until February, followed by a three-day Festival of his music at Covent Garden – a unique honour – in March. Celebrity was developing apace. He was elected to membership of the Athaneum Club, and awarded an honorary degree, his second. To cap it all, the public announcement of his knighthood came towards the end of June. Elgar received about eighty letters of congratulation by first post on 25th June, and went down to the Club to enjoy another four-ball match by way of celebration. It was the last game he played that year, and it may well be virtually the last time he played at all. In July the Elgars moved to a grand house in Hereford, and left Malvern behind them. The composer came back to the Club just once the following year, and then only to lunch, and he seems never to have visited it again, or to have shown any interest in playing golf at Hereford.

Over the next fourteen years, Lady Elgar's diary makes just a few final references to Elgar and golf. In November, 1908, shortly before the première of his First Symphony, the composer stayed with some old Malvern friends, the Jebb Scotts, at Lymington in the New Forest. After a 'long lovely drive thro' forest most beautiful,' there was an afternoon visit to the local Links; Jebb Scott had been a member of the Worcestershire Club along with Elgar. Exhausted by the preparation of his huge symphony, the composer no doubt found the visit, together with whatever golf was played, a therapeutic experience. The game must often have helped Elgar in this way, for since the Malvern days he had been subject to illness and depression, and he continued to be plagued by mysterious, and apparently worsening, health problems. There was much financial and creative anxiety attached to the purchase of a large house in London, the summit of the Elgars' social ambitions, in 1912. He tried some golf while taking a week's cure at Llandridnod in March 1913, and 'found practising golf place' on his return. There were two anxious consultations with medical men later in the month, and Alice reported on both occasions that the doctors, knowing the value of fresh air and exercise, had 'insisted on Golf.' She and Carice set off one day, with Elgar 'tired & in bed for breakfast,' to Chorley Wood 'to find nice golfing place' for him, but to no avail. Golf, like cycling, had been abandoned for good. Four years later, with no improvement in his general health, Elgar was again examined by specialists, and was again advised to resume golf. But this time the fresh air went out of the window, for they also recommended him to smoke.

It is characteristic of Elgar that although he gave up playing golf, he retained an informed interest in it until the end of his life. His nephew Martin Grafton recalled how, during the twenties and thirties, he would often meet the composer on Sundays at Bromsgrove, where his sister Polly lived. The youngster heard many of the conversations that took place, and recalled that they discussed many subjects of interest to Elgar apart from music, including money, wine, friends (including those in the 'Enigma' circle) racing, and chemistry. And golf was also on the list, for Martin recalled 'he remained almost as passionately interested in the sport as he was in horseracing. He would discuss the prospects of the latest star in the firmament at length, and since my grandmother's interest in the game was minimal to say the least, he would occasionally turn to me for audience. I thus learned a lot about golf, although at a relatively early age.'

Martin's acquisition of golfing knowledge was not matched by any marked degree of familial deference to its source. Of the photograph of Elgar playing at Stoke, he thought his uncle was playing 'the most appalling golf shot I have ever seen . . . had he been casting a fly at a trout his stance would have been pretty good but as a drive from a tee which is what I think it was supposed to be it was awful.'

*

Half-way through the First World War, when he was busy patriotically teaching marksmanship to all comers in his Oxford garden, RBT's health broke down. 'The end of the trail,' he called it. But he lived on until the end of April, 1923, publishing 'Inspired Golf' in 1921 and devoting himself also to putting his American 'Tenderfoot' books together from talks and articles, dictating from notes even in the last few weeks of his life. His death must have come as a most unpleasant surprise and shock to Elgar, who all unwittingly set off for a drive with Carice to Oxford on the first of May 1923 to call on his old golfing friend and 'Enigma' Variation. On arriving, they found that his funeral had taken place that very day.

Townshend did not allow his invalid days to get him down; the pioneer spirit, and his facility for the apt quotation never deserted him. The final chapter of his last book concludes, 'And now at the end I can say life has not been a disappointment, and there is a good deal of truth in the line: "And for His chosen, pours His best wine last!"' Surely he – and Elgar – would have echoed, too, the sentiments of P. G. Wodehouse : -

'Perhaps the most outstanding virtue of this noble pursuit is the fact that it is a medicine for the soul. Its great service to humanity is that it teaches human beings that, whatever petty triumphs they may have achieved in other walks of life, they are after all merely human.'

Appendix 1: Translations.

I am grateful to David Gosden, former colleague, and friend, and himself a Cambridge Classics scholar, for permission to reprint his response to my request for enlightenment over RBT's quotations from the Latin, both in the text of *Inspired Golf* and in his letters to Elgar. As a result I am tempted to claim that we will have a better understanding of such points than the composer himself, whose acquaintance with classical languages was something less than close, however much at times he may not have been averse to giving a contrary impression.

*

'Dear Kevin, nothing is ever simple to translate! However:

Page 21. *Propria quae maribus.* If I ever knew the quotation, I've forgotten it now! I thought maybe it was from Caesar's Gallic Wars – the every-schoolboy-has-done-it job. But it seems not to be from the famous opening pages. Silly idea that was! The word order etc. make it almost certainly from a poem. I still have no idea of the source. Shorn of a context, it means something like - [Things] which [are] peculiar to the seas [like whales?]

Page 21. *Pons Asinorum* used to be well-used – for any thing that is likely to trip the uninformed or something like that. Originally it was said (one is told) of Euclid's Fifth proposition, *which beginners, etc. **, find difficulty in "getting over"* - the literal meaning of the phrase being "Bridge of asses." [Here I have quoted from S.O.D.] You'll be excited to know the contents of Euclid's Fifth Proposition, and possibly surprised that it was deemed to be such a difficult bridge to cross:

The angles at the base of an isosceles triangle are equal to one another; and if the equal sides be produced the angles on the other side of the base shall be equal to one another.

Aha! But that was in Book 1. There are Other Books. In Book II, Prop.5 is:

If a straight line be divided into two equal parts and also into two unequal parts, the rectangle contained by the unequal parts, together with the square on the line between the points of section, is equal to the square of half the line

You can include me among the asses. And there are Fifth Propositions (I presume) in the remaining books, at least as far as Book XI!

** I like the "etc." Not just "beginners", presumably?

Page 21. Presumably *cadit quaestio* had its home in legal circles: "The question falls", something like 'No case . . .' I guess that the idea is that there is no "case" or "question" to "answer" owing to a now-discovered inherent gap or mistake in the assumptions behind the case or question.'

Page 55. *Potes quia posse videris* is definitely a touch enigmatic. One Latin word can actually serve several grammatical purposes (cf. English "strikes" can be verb or noun). I first supposed *videris* was either Future Perfect Indicative (literally "you will have seen") or Perfect Subjunctive (untranslatable). Shows how rusty I am! But now I recall a third and simpler possibility! The PRESENT PASSIVE of "video" goes like this:

Videor
Videris
Videtur
Videmur
Videmini
Videntur

It's got to be this, not what I first thought. Now "videor" etc besides meaning "I am seen," also, and probably much more commonly, means "*I seem"* ! I still can't make much sense of the quote, but I think we have to work on the lines of "You are able because you seem to be able." I haven't the original context in front of me now, - maybe that will shed light. Something like "People perceive* you as able, so in effect you are able . . ." Remember that Gilbertian fun in *The Mikado* between Poo-Bah and co. and the Mikado? "When your Majesty says, 'Let a thing be done,' it's as good as done," etc. [* Note the allusion to the current fad for one's "perceptions"!]

Page 58. *Macte . . . virtute* seemed familiar [I *ought* to have recognised it at once], and I looked it up in my mammoth Latin dictionary – the kind that gives lots of examples of the word-in-use. There it was, a long entry about "Macte" – something of a curio grammatically – I won't weary you with the technicalities. The book says: 'With or without *esto* [Be thou . . .!] an applauding or congratulatory exclamation addressed to men.' [!!] This restriction may reflect the fact that normally "macte virtute" occurs as a unit and *virtus* must mean "man-liness" (and courage or virtue derivatively). The dictionary offers as typical interpretations, 'Bravo! Hail to thee! Well done! That's right! Go on!' The phrase is used in all literary genres from letters to odes. But the best is yet to be. Among the citations is your actual sentence! 'Macte nova virtute, puer; sic itur ad astra.' And my edition of Vergil has generous notes. For this passage it gives a straightforward translation, without comment. 'Blessings on thy young prowess, my son; this is the path to heaven.'

Reviewing your letter and Townshend's, I realise that the *Macte virtute* quote was meant to stand in for the 'native Irish' and is roughly equivalent of 'More power to your elbow' or 'Do go ahead, my dear fellow,' or 'Hurrah,' – or all three! As for the point of this strange remark of Vergil's in *Aeneid IX* - it comes late in the story of Aeneas, long after he had escaped from the flames of Troy and after he had dallied with Dido – I assume he is battling with the natives of Italy. But I gather that the passage is full of veiled references to the events of Vergil's own day, the Emperor Augustus and all that (whose court poet V. was)

We can excuse ourselves from further probing. The Notes say, 'The reference, expressed with oracular* obscurity, is to the settlement of Augustus.' *Amen, say I. But it would be nice to know who the implied youth is. Augustus' heir? To puzzle out exactly how this *Macte virtute* stuff functions in the fight-with-the-Italians context in the *Aeneid* is beyond me, I'm afraid. I wonder if former generations of classically educated persons actually carried all this stuff in their heads and could instantly 'apply' the message . . .'

Page 73. *Maxima debetur puero reverentia* – "The greatest respect is owed (due) to the boy" – presumably the generic boy, not any individual. Sheer "child-centred education" sloppiness!'

Appendix 2. A Note on Elgar's Golf Clubs.

As has been said, it would appear that on leaving Malvern for Hereford in 1904, Elgar had no intention of seeking out further opportunities to play golf. He gave his clubs to Florence Burley, a sister of Rosa Burley, the headmistress of the boarding school in Malvern which Carice attended, and a close confidante of the composer. The donation of the clubs may be a measure of just how much golf was connected in Elgar's mind with the undulating old course dominated by the Hills; playing somewhere else would never be the same. Part of the subsequent history of Elgar's clubs is given in this letter from Rosa and Florence's brother Ernest, who, forty years on, returned the clubs with their 'drain-pipe' caddy-bag, so that Carice could include them among the artefacts in the Museum dedicated to her father's memory which she had done so much to set up.

> Gelsmoor,
> Rothley,
> Leics
>
> August 4th, 1944

Dear Madam,

I forwarded the golf clubs yesterday, after giving them a certain amount of cleaning & hope they will arrive safely. I should be glad if you would kindly return the holdall wrapper, as I have found it a very useful possession. The clubs with the caddy were originally given to my youngest sister Florence, by Mr Elgar, as he then was, & before she went out to Johannesburg, she left them in my charge. My nephew George Farras was staying with me at the school-house, Bolsover, Chesterfield, and on one occasion borrowed the clubs for a practice on a piece of rough ground & by a clumsy shot managed to break the staff of one of the clubs. I set to work and wrapped the shaft almost its entire length. It is quite an amateur piece of work & I was tempted to send the club to a professional to repair it properly, but on second thoughts decided not to do so, as that wrapping is a certain identification. I am glad to be able to send them to the place where they should be and remain.

Yours very faithfully,

Ernest A Burley.

Elgar's clubs do indeed remain at the Museum at Broadheath, near Worcester, together with the brass buttons that Dora Penny remembered so well from the composer's red golf blazer and what Ernest Burley described as his 'caddy-bag.' This is an example of 'The Automaton Caddie,' a new design ('Patent applied for') by Osmond's of London with a built-in stand, which appeared in the early eighteen-nineties. Presumably it was more economic proposition for a hard-pressed music teacher than endlessly tipping the Club's caddy-boys. It contains just three clubs, all with hickory shafts wound with leather grips; a wooden driver, its club face reinforced with horn and lead weights, perhaps the 'new driver' that Elgar acquired during his golfing holiday at Bournemouth in 1897; and two irons. One, a mashie, the one broken by George Farras, is bound round with twine, a 'certain identification,' as Ernest Burley said, and the other, approximating to a modern No. 2, was presumably used by Elgar as a putter.

Acknowledgements

My first thanks come sadly too late for their recipient, who died during the writing of this book. It was Jim Bennett, then Curator of the Elgar Birthplace Museum, who kindly gave me access to Elgar's own copy of *Inspired Golf* over ten years ago, and thus sowed the seeds of this project. I remain most grateful to him for this and the many other research opportunities he made so easily possible. His genial, hospitable welcomes to Rose Cottage remain fresh in the memory.

I would also like to thank Claud Powell for sharing his interest in RBT with me, thus sparking off my own. Alan Bennett MBE and his wife Pat generously permitted me full access to their Catalogue of the Elgar Archive, making it a straightforward matter to trace the letters from which I have quoted. For access to these letters, and permission to reproduce them, together with Elgar's typescript memorandum on golf and the photographs of the composer playing at Stoke Prior and Hasfield, and other material, I am grateful to Cathy Sloan, Curator of the Birthplace Museum, and the Elgar Will Trust. For further kind help at the Birthplace I thank Chris Bennett and Margaret Saunders, Archivist. I have also gratefully used material from Dr. Percy Young's *Elgar OM* (second edition), his *Letters and Other Writings of Edward Elgar,* and from *Edward Elgar, Letters of a Lifetime,* edited by Dr J. N. Moore.

Alan Bennett has also kindly enlivened the text with his cartoons. For other illustrations I am indebted to Peter Norbury, Roger Hall-Jones, (who most kindly provided material from *The Illustrated Sporting and Dramatic News* of October 1900), to the British Library for the photographs from *The Sketch* of October, 1903, and to Garnet Scott for permitting the reproduction of photographs from his excellent *Centenary History of the Worcestershire Golf Club* (Malvern, 1979). I have gratefully plundered this book for background information on the WGC in Elgar's day, and can only hope that I have accurately represented his research. I would like to further thank Mr Scott for most kindly sharing his evaluation of Elgar's caddy-bag and golf clubs on display at the Elgar Museum, and Jacqueline Howe, who welcomed me to the WGC's magnificent new Club house and encouraged an inspection of the archives.

The photograph of the two bars of music 'made probably on the golf links' is reproduced from *David Ffrangçon-Davies: His Life And Book,* by Marjorie Ffrangçon-Davies.

David Gosden and Peter Smith have both given generously of their time and expertise. For their ready help in guiding me towards records of the Oxford University Golf Club I wish to thank Stephen Tomlinson of the Bodleian Library, Robert Simpson, Peter Bathurst, Donald Steel, John Uzielli, and J. R. Gillum. David Holmes, the Oxford University Registrar, and his secretary Jeanne Gurr most kindly made it possible to for me to study the OUGC Minute Books at the University Offices, Wellington Square. I am most grateful to Jennifer Grafton for permission to reproduce anecdotes given by Martin Grafton in a talk to the West Midlands Branch of the Elgar Society, and thank Michael Trott and Geoffrey Bradshaw for their help in this respect.

The quotations from Alice Elgar's Diary have been verified from the copy held at the Worcestershire Public Record Office. I am grateful for the opportunity of quoting passages from *The Heart of a Goof* by P. G. Wodehouse, published by Hutchinson, reprinted by permission of The Random House Group Ltd, and A.P.Watt Ltd on behalf of the Trustees of the Wodehouse Estate. Any omission of copyright acknowledgement is regretted and will be rectified in future editions.

Game Abandoned

Tracing the Elgar roots?

Where better to stay than
The Cottage in the Wood Hotel

Perched high up on the Malvern Hills where Elgar loved to walk and bicycle, is The Cottage in the Wood Hotel and Restaurant with the same breathtaking thirty mile views so admired by the great composer.

He lived down the hill below us for a time and is buried at St. Wulstan's with his wife and daughter, just along the road.

Thirty-one bedrooms, nineteen of which are in our sumptuous new building 'The Pinnacles', two AA Rosette food and a 600+ wine list.

Short break rates available virtually all year.

The Cottage in the Wood

Holywell Road, Malvern Wells,
Worcestershire, WR14 4LG
Tel: (01684) 575859
Fax: (01684) 560662
www.cottageinthewood.co.uk

The Worcestershire Golf Club

Wood Farm, Malvern Wells, Worcs, WR14 4PP
Tel: 01684 575992

Secretary: Jacqueline Howe

Nestling comfortably on the eastern side of the Malvern Hills, The Worcestershire Golf Club can lay claim to being the oldest Club in the Midlands. The course was originally 12 holes when golf was played on Malvern Common, until 1925 when the Club moved to its current location at Wood Farm.

The course in its present form is a fair test of any golfer's ability and scenically it would be hard to find one more aesthetically pleasing.

Visitors will be assured a warm welcome from our friendly team of staff.

Group bookings accepted.
Please telephone
01684 575992 for details

Or visit our web site
www.theworcestershiregolfclub.co.uk

The Elgar Birthplace Museum

Visit Elgar's historic Birthplace Cottage and the modern Elgar Centre for a fascinating insight into the life and music, family and friends, inspirations and musical development of one of England's greatest composers.

See Elgar's 100 year-old golf clubs and the Osmond patented *Automaton Caddie* in the Hobbies Room at the Elgar Birthplace Museum.

And much more...

- *Follow the audio tour and sample his music - Salut d'Amour and the symphonies, church music and chamber works, concertos and choral masterpieces, part-songs and Pomp and Circumstance.*

- *See his gramophone, and the desk laid out as Elgar's wife Alice used to prepare it for him.*

- *Discover Elgar's family and social life; his travels; and his hobbies, from golf to science.*

Crown East Lane, Lower Broadheath, Worcester WR2 6RH
Tel: 01905 333224   Fax: 01905 333426
Web: www.elgarmuseum.org   Email: info@elgarmuseum.org
3 miles west of Worcester, sign posted off A44 Worcester/Leominster Road.
Open daily 11am - 5pm (last adm. 4.15pm)